TOBRUK
COMMANDO

The Raid to Destroy
Rommel's Base

Gordon Landsborough

Frontline Books

Tobruk Commando: The Raid to Destroy Rommel's Base

A Greenhill Book

First published in 1989 by Greenhill Books, Lionel Leventhal Limited
www.greenhillbooks.com

This paperback edition published in 2015 by

Frontline Books
an imprint of Pen & Sword Books Ltd,
47 Church Street, Barnsley, S. Yorkshire, S70 2AS
For more information on our books, please visit
www.frontline-books.com, email info@frontline-books.com
or write to us at the above address.

Copyright © Gordon Landsborough, 1956
Introduction © David List, 1989

The right of Gordon Landsborough to be identified as the author of this
work has been asserted by him in accordance with the Copyright, Designs
and Patents Act 1988.

ISBN: 978-1-84832-244-8

CIP data records for this title are available from the British Library

Publishing History
Tobruk Commando was first published in 1956 (Cassell & Co. Ltd) and is reproduced
here as the original edition, with a new Introduction by David List.

Printed and bound by CPI Group (UK) Ltd, Croydon, CR0 4YY

ACKNOWLEDGEMENT AND NOTE

A work such as *Tobruk Commando* could never be prepared without considerable co-operation from participants and from various official bodies. To thank all who have assisted me in my task would require pages of acknowledgement, and there are elements against such a course.

I would, however, like to record my appreciation of the assistance accorded by all Regiments named in this book, by the Admiralty, War Office, Cabinet Office and Imperial War Museum.

To the dozens of survivors from Operation Agreement who displayed such magnificent patience in the face of what surely must have been tedious questioning, may I say, 'Thank you. I am glad to have met you all.' And please forgive no greater acknowledgement of your kindness than that.

The only names of personnel engaged in Operation Agreement that I have altered are those of the S.I.G., this at the request of the War Office in the interests of Security.

Also at the request of the War Office, I must make it clear that opinions and conclusions proffered or implied are mine and have no official sanction.

Gordon Landsborough

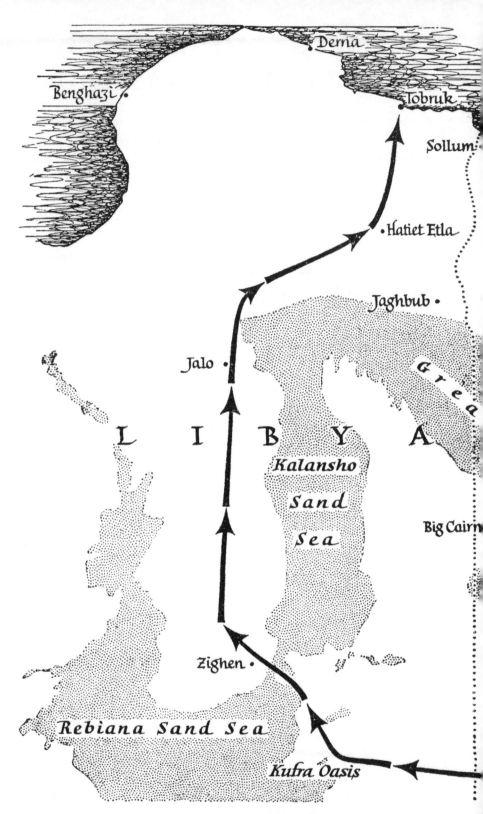

Benghazi •

Derna •

Tobruk •

Sollum •

• Hatiet Etla

Jaghbub •

Jalo •

Grea

L I B Y A

Kalansho

Sand

Sea

Big Cairn

Zighen •

Rebiana Sand Sea

Kufra Oasis

SHOWING THE ROUTE TO TOBRUK TAKEN

The Western Desert

N

Matrûh

Alexandria

El Alamein

Cairo

Qattara
Depression

El Faiyûm

wa
sis

R. Nile

E G Y P T

El Minya

Easy Ascent' •'Ain Dalla

Asyût

nd sea

Dakhla Oasis

El Khârga

Kharga
Oasis

0 ——— 100 ——— 200 miles (approximate)

NEW INTRODUCTION

In many ways this is a remarkable work with an eye for detail, quality of description and air of mystery that is as fresh, immediate, intriguing and compelling to the public of the late 1980s as it was to its original readership in 1956 since so many of its loose ends remain tantalisingly un-resolved.

Relating as it does the story of a major British tri-service operation in the Western Desert during September 1942, both from the viewpoints of participants', in what the West now chooses to call 'Unconventional Military Forces' or 'Special Forces', as well as that of the Royal Navy units that supported them, it is a vividly evocative account based on contemporary sources and individual interviews of a tragic affair that went seriously awry with the total loss of the AA cruiser *HMS Coventry*, the Tribal Class destroyers *HMS Sikh* and *Zulu*, 2 MLs, 3 MTBs, *MTB 314* operational in enemy hands, the death or capture of 300 Royal Marines of the 11th Battalion, Royal Marines, landed in the wrong place, and the destruction of D Squadron, 1 Special Service Regiment and the S.I.G. as fighting units after they had captured all their initial objectives following a daring and very risky infiltration, under the guidance of Y1 Patrol, Long Range Desert Group.

Quite why Operation Agreement went sour is still a matter of debate amongst historians. At this distance in time, with the malleability of memory, the records released for public inspection, partial, incomplete or contradictory, and a trail of published works drawing, uncritically all too often, on sources which in some cases have been demons-trably 'economical with the truth' to muddy the waters even further, it is increasingly unlikely that any finally satisfactory attribution of cause and effect will ever be reached.

It would be fair to say, however, that the balance of evidence from German records alone indicates that the unusual strength and duration of the air attack on Tobruk on 13 September 1942 was the major contributing factor for the alertness of German rear area defence units on that night, and that preparations for a 'landing alert' signal were made by Generalmajor Deindl at 2300 hours, i.e. some two hours after the commencement of the diversionary air raids, and well after the commandos had neutralised their first targets.

Available Italian records on the matter are beset by so many difficulties of factual interpretation as to make sensible comment on the issue from this perspective problematic at present. A report by the New Zealand Brigadier Clifton on an Italian 'stool pigeon' introduced into his prison well before the raids, who knew the dates of the upcoming operations, but not their full extent, does not seem to have been followed up in the British investigations into the aftermath of the raids, and remains yet one more unresolved aspect of Italian foreknowledge of the Special Forces raids.

This said, Landsborough's grasp and integration of the complex events of that fateful September can be little faulted when dealing with the land actions; his grip of the naval details is less sure. (Interested readers are referred to the 1987 work of naval historian, Peter C. Smith, in his *Massacre at Tobruk* for a better researched account of the naval and Royal Marine side of Operation Agreement. It should be noted, however, that his treatment of the commando details is inconsistent in many respects and not comparable with Landsborough's).

In practically all aspects of the commando story Landsborough is congruent with the official British reports of the time, and the recorded memories of participants' in later years.

In his 'acknowledgement and note' Landsborough states he has altered the names of the S.I.G. personnel 'at the request of the War Office in the interests of Security'. There are now no tenable grounds for observing this request, the true names of these very brave men having been revealed in several published works, as well as being easily obtainable from the relevant records open to the public under the Public Records Act. Accordingly, readers will be interested to know that the 'Special Identification Group' was actually designated the Special Interrogation Group, a sub-unit of D Squadron, 1 Special Service Regiment, with a full strength of 21 men, and that 'Captain Herbert Bray, late of the 4th Indian Division' was Captain Herbert Cecil Buck, MC, 3/1 Punjabis who, although wounded, survived the raid and after a period as a POW was later accepted for service in the SAS preparing for operations in the Far East in 1945.

'Lieutenant David Lanark' was Lieutenant David Russell, Scots Guards, who was subsequently murdered in Yugoslavia for the gold he was carrying on a Special Operations Executive operation running into Rumania in August 1943.

Corporal Steiner (also shown as Kennedy in some records) was Corporal Hillman who later saw service with 1 SAS.

Privates Berg and Weizmann were, respectively, Roer and Opprower, whilst Private Wilenski was probably H. Goldstein, who was also on the Mersah-Matruh and Fuka raids with L Detachment. He survived Operation Agreement as a POW and also volunteered with Buck for the SAS going to the Far East in 1945.

Finally, it is also worth noting, that of the two S.I.G. turn-coats 'Esser' and 'Brückner' both were recruited via the Combined Services Detailed Interrogation Centre, having been captured from 361 Afrika Regiment (which had a high proportion of ex Foreign Legion men) and that the name 'Brückner' is known to be a pseudonym for his real name, Brockmann. It is probable that the name 'Esser' was also false, both the result of a known CSDIC practice of providing new identities for captured or surrendered enemy personnel who agreed to act as 'double agents' for the

Allies.

So many of the mysteries of Operation Agreement remain to be unravelled, if unravelled they ever can be. Landsborough firmly attributes the original idea for a stealthy infiltration, 'shoot and scoot' type mission, using classic Special Forces operational technique, to John Haseldon, with numerous unnamed interests inflating the idea out of all proportion to its worth.

Sir David Hunt, a highly reputable Intelligence officer at GHQ, Cairo attributes the concept to Herbert Buck in a work published in 1966, complete with various strictures on the inadequacies of the Desert 'Private Armies', not all of which are borne out by official files.

Records publically available in the 1980s are equivocal on the matter. Readers are invited to read on, and judge for themselves, the merits of Landsborough's case, and to enjoy, above all, a masterly crafted, yet essentially true, mystery story.

DAVID LIST, 1989

I

FOR Y1 Patrol of the Long Range Desert Group, Operation Agreement began on August 23, 1942. That was the day they moved out of Abbassieh Barracks, Cairo, and headed for the L.R.D.G. base in Faiyum.

It began well. It was the custom for patrols to have a farewell lunch together before taking to the desert again, and this day, with their vehicles and themselves re-equipped for a long trek behind the enemy lines, they did themselves proud in a café near the Continental Hotel.

Perhaps they drank too much. If they did, their commander, Captain Lloyd Owen, turned an indulgent eye upon the proceedings, and enjoyed himself no less than his patrol of twenty men. He was young himself—just twenty-four—a regular Army officer with an understanding of men. He knew that for the next month or two his patrol would be living under conditions of acute discomfort, with a constant threat to their lives the moment they turned their unsuspecting enemy's flank, and so it was natural that they should seize this last chance of a taste of Cairo pleasures before taking to the desert again.

A friendly dignitary from the British Embassy saw the Arab-head-dressed British troopers in the café and joined them for a drink. When they left, the Embassy official left with them; when they mounted their six open patrol cars, he took his place on the piled-up kit and surveyed Cairo benevolently from an angle not usual for Embassy dignitaries. And Cairo surveyed him.

Conditions worsened—or improved—at the first set of traffic lights. They turned red and the convoy of desert-camouflaged Chevrolets halted. A gunner on the first

truck decided for some reason that the trucks had become
bogged down in soft sand, and he at once leapt off, got out
the sand channels, and went through the drill for freeing
sand-held vehicles. Twenty comrades and a benign
Embassy official encouraged him with loud advice which
brought the crowded Cairo pavements' interest upon them.

The lights changed, and the trucks careered gaily off,
their wild-looking, many-bearded occupants drawing the
envy of thousands of more discipline-bound, conventionally
attired Allied troops in Cairo.

It was a good start to their patrol. True, there was an
awkward moment outside the Embassy when the well lit-up
official was decanted upon the broad steps under the brooding
gaze of a superior; but that was no concern of the L.R.D.G.

In riotous mood, intent upon a last fling, they travelled
south, out of Cairo until they came to the Pyramids. As
the mighty tombs grew larger to their cheerful if slightly
bemused eyes, all looked at them and felt that Something
Must Be Done About Them. It was impossible this day
to pass the Pyramids without in some way paying tribute to
a civilization which had also had its moments in the desert.

The great idea came to them. Afterwards there were
some who thought it was Captain Lloyd Owen's contribution to the day's festivities. Whoever's idea it was, Mena
was soon startled to see six L.R.D.G. patrol cars rocketing
round the Pyramids at crazy speed while coloured Verey
lights cascaded in great brilliance over them.

Next moment, or so it seemed to the patrol, the area was
stiff with military policemen. Not ordinarily stern-looking
M.P.s either, but a sweating bunch of red-faced running
men with trouble in their grim eyes and hoarse threats in
their shouting voices. The cars stopped. The patrol was
surrounded by an enemy more to be feared than a panzer
corps. Red Caps shoved belligerent faces at the truculent
occupants and demanded to know who was in charge of
the party.

The smallest man present was unanimously elected for
the rôle. He was Lloyd Owen's own driver, a tough little

Somerset farmer called Trooper Cave. He accepted responsibility in tones unusual before M.P.s, and he also added his opinion of Red Caps, and what he thought of them was interesting but of no value in terms of diplomacy.

When the proceedings had reached a lively stage, Lloyd Owen came up with his rank and was pounced upon by the smarting, outraged Military Police.

' Where do you think you're going?' a sergeant demanded unpleasantly.

Lloyd Owen thought it over. Then he said, 'Tripoli.' It was as good a place as any, and not too inexact at that.

The Military Police, rightly placing Tripoli, in Tripolitania, a thousand-odd miles to the rear of Rommel's forward line at Alamein, took exception to the reply and invited Captain Lloyd Owen to step into the Military Police office and discuss the matter in greater detail. Still suffused with the glow that follows an excellent lunch eaten in the best of company, Lloyd Owen went with them, leaving his desert warriors to make further comments upon military police that certainly did nothing to improve relations. . . .

Next morning, the day their big trek really started, Y1 Patrol felt bad. Their heads ached, their eyes were heavy and winced against the hot, reflecting sun that burned into their camp at the Faiyum; throats were unnaturally parched and there was a feeling that things might have been rather overdone a little the previous day.

But added to their physical discomfort was an unease borne of a memory of irate Military Police the night before. They were in trouble, the whole patrol from Captain Lloyd Owen down to—and very much down to—Trooper Cave. They knew that the matter of Verey-lighted Pyramids was to come up before their C.O. shortly, and though they had every confidence in him, though they knew he was a most tolerant and understanding officer, they also knew he would have to do something about the charges.

The men discussed the matter so far as their depression permitted. All agreed that the situation would be eased if they got clear out of Egypt for a month or so; perhaps the thing might even blow over during that time, they thought, brightening. So they watched, with something like impatience, the curving, hard-baked mud track that ran from the Faiyum to the Nile road that led to Cairo; they waited for sight of a dust cloud that would tell of an approaching convoy, their charges for the next weeks.

The L.R.D.G. patrol had no idea what their job was to be, nor even their destination. Only Lloyd Owen knew and he would not tell his men until he was able to do so.

But that was a usual condition attached to operations with the L.R.D.G. To an outsider it smacked of cloak-and-dagger work, but the blasé desert travellers, as nomadic as any tribe of Bedouins, never questioned the arrangement. There was a war on. Rommel was pressing a barely-held line which went through an obscure Arab village named El Alamein. Militarily, British fortunes in the Middle East were about as low as they could be. Secrecy was vital to many of the plans which involved the L.R.D.G.

All they had been informed was that a commando* would come into their camp from the direction of Cairo; they, the L.R.D.G., would guide the commando into the desert to some distant map reference and leave it there. The L.R.D.G. did understand, however, that for once their part in the operation would be minor—this time the cloak-and-dagger work would come from the commando.

Even for the L.R.D.G., conducting a commando into the desert was something unusual. Agents, one or two at a time, yes. But not a commando. As they hung around the mobile office vehicles of the L.R.D.G. camp, their six sand-camouflaged vehicles drawn up in line ready for instant departure, they must have speculated about the mysterious commando, must have wondered at the work it was to do, and how it fitted into the scheme of things so far as a defeated desert army was concerned.

* Throughout this book 'commando' is used in its original sense, meaning a small, highly mobile striking force ; this even though, as will be seen, this particular commando embraced sappers, signallers and gunners, apart from Middle East Commando-trained personnel.

Perhaps, too, with the intolerance of experts, they felt faintly antagonistic towards their as yet unknown charges: the deep desert, they felt, was *their* domain, and they did not welcome trespassers into their purely private battlefield.

The L.R.D.G. were, by conventional standards, rather a weird-looking lot, and there was no doubt that there were moments when they tended to dramatize themselves and their work, and their feeling of superiority towards all other desert warriors was not always tactfully concealed.

But they were good; even the envious had to admit it. They were an élite corps, rightly proud of their achievements, rightly jealous of their new and scintillating reputation.

The Long Range Desert Group had grown out of the peace-time desert explorations of enthusiasts stationed or living in Egypt, men like Major R. A. Bagnold, Captain G. L. Prendergast, and an archæologist, W. B. Kennedy Shaw. They had learned to traverse the inhospitable wastelands of the great Egyptian desert in Model T and Model A Fords, marking safe ways through vast, shifting sand seas which engulfed everything trying to move over them, finding waterholes known only to nomadic tribes, and living where even Arabs could not have existed.

With the beginning of the Wavell campaigns in the northern desert, the experience of these explorers was recognized, and Major Bagnold was commissioned to organize a Long Range Desert Group. By August, 1942, it had been in existence roughly two years, but in that time it had acquired a reputation that was fabulous; to wear the L.R.D.G. shoulder-tabs in Cairo was to be accorded a respect that amounted almost to deference by Eighth Army, itself no mean desert campaigner.

The L.R.D.G. patrols probed hundreds of miles behind the enemy lines, acting in many rôles but always acquitting themselves well. They built a chain of supply points across the desert, so that they could extend their effective radius of operation to fantastic distances, and they continually harassed and worried an enemy who never took to the desert in the same way as our British, Rhodesian and New Zealand L.R.D.G.

But while quite willing to bask in the praise and special regard that came their way (what élite corps wouldn't?) they would be the last to declare their work glamorous or exciting. They had reduced desert campaigning to something very ordinary. To be a member of the L.R.D.G., they would tell you, meant you had to be less of a hero than a man able to stand up to incredible physical hardships, while at the same time suffering a loneliness of existence which few British soldiers were ever called upon to bear.

Long Range Desert work meant weeks, often months, away from contact with other men. It meant rarely washing, rarely shaving, living in sweat-saturated clothes that could be cleaned only when the patrol ended. It meant living rough, sleeping in the sand beside their vehicles, and at all times exposed to the driving desert winds and the fierce, torrid, near-tropical Sahara sun.

It was the sun that was killing. Often they would be exposed to it in their open 30-cwt. Chevrolets from six in the morning until eight or nine at night. Long days; days of monotony and discomfort beyond normal endurance. But the most sapping, morale-destroying feature of life in the desert was the agonizing, never-satiated thirst promoted by the sun and arid surroundings. The normal day's ration of water for a patrol was four pints per head, out of which they had to contribute their share to the day's cooking. Thirst was their constant companion; their mugful of tea or water in the middle of the day or at evening was something their straining imaginations welcomed for hours before the event.

Patrols were often uneventful—but not always. Sometimes, perhaps carrying mysterious Allied agents into the Jebel or other enemy-occupied territory, they would run into a German or Italian column of transport. Depending on its size, they would tear in, shooting it up and destroying it completely, thereby creating alarm in an enemy which never expected to find their opponents so far from the front line. And sometimes the L.R.D.G. would storm a lonely outpost and wipe it out.

Probably, however, the L.R.D.G.'s greatest contribution to an eventual Allied victory in the desert was their Road Watch. For months on end, never relaxing for a day, the L.R.D.G. kept watch on the main Axis supply road at Marble Arch, two hundred miles west of Benghazi, logging all troop movements and radioing back reports to Cairo. It was unspectacular. It was the chore most hated by the L.R.D.G., but it was fine Intelligence work and of incalculable value to the Desert Army.

The Road Watch had been Y1 Patrol's last duty. Five or six weeks of agonizing desert travel, then two weeks lying on their stomachs staring at enemy transport only a few hundred yards from their hide-out.

At least, they thought, guiding the commando would be less boring than the Road Watch. . . .

Someone said something and pointed. The desert commando could be seen in the distance, a rising cloud of dust that crawled with painful slowness towards the oasis of Faiyum. Captain Lloyd Owen came down the steps of the mobile office vehicle and stood where he could receive the commando on their arrival. His men began to stir, picking up their odds and ends of equipment and getting ready for the drive out.

Mostly they were bearded. That was a mark that distinguished them from most units—bearded British soldiers. For what was the sense in shaving between patrols if lack of water caused them to go through the tickly process of rebearding each time they disappeared into the desert? And they wore the flowing *kafir* head-dress of the desert Arab. Affectation? A desire to be out of the ordinary? Perhaps. But a useful affectation: there was nothing like it for protecting necks from the hot slanting rays of the sun; and when the wind blew and skirled up the biting, needle-sharp sand-grains, a *kafir* wrapped around the face was a protection against discomfort better than anything else. In the desert, so far as head-dresses were concerned, the Arab knew best.

Eight trucks—open British Army 3-tonners—seemed suddenly to drive out of the dust cloud of their own creation and began the ascent of the ridge on which the L.R.D.G. base was situated.   The L.R.D.G. came to the entrances of their tents and looked out, interested in spite of a pessimism born of a hangover, wanting to see the mysterious commando.

The eight trucks slowed, entering the camp, then came to a halt in line on the roadway just beyond Captain Lloyd Owen.   The L.R.D.G. saw men perched on the metal sides and tailboards of the trucks (a crime according to Middle East Orders of the time, but the Desert Army went on sitting on truck sides because there was really nowhere else to sit inside open lorries).   There were seventy-three officers and men in the commando.

The L.R.D.G., no cissies themselves, saw a tough-looking mob jump from the wagons; even the officers had that air of vigour and drive which goes with commando-training.

For the most part the commando looked big—bigger, fitter and more muscular than the average trooper.   And biggest of all was a giant squadron sergeant-major, who must have topped six feet by several inches.   There were plenty of flat noses and thick ears among the party, and though at this moment they were cheerful, boisterous, and certainly anything but aggressive, there was something in their manner which said they could be rough boys if driven to it.

No one drove them to it.   Not at that moment, anyway. Without orders, each truck set up a can of petrol-soaked sand and began to boil water.   Always there was tea at every stop on a desert trek.

Two of the officers with the commando wore kilts.   The leader, a tall, erect major, wore the Hodden Grey kilt of the London Scottish.   He descended from the leading truck, smiling as he approached the L.R.D.G. patrol commander.

Lloyd Owen knew him—they had been in on planning together.   More, he knew the curious composition of this intriguing little commando.

About half were real commandos, officers and men of the recently disbanded Middle East Commando unit. They had been transferred into another irregular force upon disbandment, the Special Services—or S.S., to give it its more usual and sinister abbreviation. The S.S. had been formed for special desert duties, for which the former Middle East Commandos were excellent material.

Almost immediately upon joining the 1st S.S. Squadron, there had been a call for volunteers for a special operation. Out of the whole Squadron which had immediately stepped forward, thirty-eight N.C.O.s and men and seven officers had been chosen.

The rest of the commando, happily brewing up in the sunshine of El Faiyum, were attached personnel, the kind of men always to be found in a largish operation. Signallers, sappers, gunners, volunteers all and fit, picked men.

But two were not soldiers. Two had pink faces and wore little round naval caps. The caps and the pink knees had amused the S.S. at first, but also puzzled them, for they could see no reason why sailors should be taken deep into the desert.

It was a curious, assorted bunch. But later there were to be some even more astonishing additions to the party.

Conversations with the commando party at this and later halts revealed that the men in it, including most of the officers, were in ignorance of their objective. But that was a usual state of affairs in operations of this kind.

In due time, when the commando had had its 'chai' and was refreshed, a process known to the Army as 'embussing' took place. Everyone climbed back on to the piled-up kit (strapped or roped down wherever possible) on the 3-ton Chevs preparatory to moving off again.

The L.R.D.G. went to their vehicles. Because of operational needs, which demanded an ability to fight without delay, using their vehicles as mobile gun platforms, the 30-cwt. Chevs each carried only two men besides the driver. A machine-gun was always mounted and instantly ready for action. Three men per truck—much more comfortable than nine or ten per vehicle. The L.R.D.G. vehicles carried a load of about two tons of petrol, water and ammunition. All the same, this was nothing like the load of kit, arms, ammunition and explosives that bedded the steel floors of the bigger Chevrolets, and accordingly the L.R.D.G. could travel at far greater speed than the 3-tonners.

Perhaps it was for this reason, then, that the L.R.D.G. simply shot ahead and soon disappeared from sight of the commando convoy at the resumption of the journey. Probably Lloyd Owen saw no reason for loitering with the slower trucks, and went off at speed to make the next halt a long one for his suffering, faintly-dispirited warriors. In any event, though the L.R.D.G. were supposed to be guides to the commando, at least for the next section of their journey there was no possibility of its getting lost: there was only one road up the Nile bank, and that was straight enough and easy to follow.

It was easy to follow, but somehow the commando smashed a 3-tonner on a raised section of roadway between well-irrigated fields. The truck suddenly swerved, charged the edge of the road and disappeared down the short embankment. The rest of the convoy slapped on its brakes and came to a skidding halt, while the men shouted, then vaulted from their trucks and went racing back to pick up the bits.

The Chev was on its side down the embankment, two wheels still spinning futilely. There was a scene of disorder on the cultivated strip below, with most of the truck's contents thrown out along with the occupants of the vehicle. The running men saw their comrades dragging themselves out of rich black mud. The language was lurid. Miraculously, no one was killed, and a few bruises amounted to nothing in that commando.

There was a hasty inspection of the overturned vehicle. 'U/S,' was the instant decision of the experts. 'We'll leave it for the L.R.D.G. to collect,' it was decided, and the men divided themselves, with salvaged equipment, over the remaining seven 3-tonners. It appeared that an officer had just taken over the wheel from a regular driver, and he was a shamed man, not able to account for the curious lapse.

The accident scarcely affected the spirits of the commando. What was a 3-ton truck in their lives? They had seen thousands shot up and destroyed in the long desert battles; they didn't worry over one abandoned vehicle. But it made the remaining trucks uncomfortably crowded, and even more heavily weighted with gear.

The drive along the Nile road was resumed. Men settled down to heat, boredom, and flies when they ran into the Egyptian riverside villages. But morale was high; the men were eager, ready for anything.

But nothing happened for the rest of their journey that day. Nothing—except one puzzling little incident.

It occurred at their first halt after leaving the Faiyum. While tea was brewing, attention was suddenly drawn to the curious conduct of a big, rugged-faced gunner officer who wore the washed-out blue shirt more usually affected by Indian or New Zealand troops.

He was sitting on the edge of an irrigation channel, brooding and remote from the rest. As they watched, they saw him take something from the right-hand pocket of his khaki drill shorts, heft it for a second and then hurl it with a splash into the water. The operation was repeated, this time with an object taken from the left pocket. Intrigued, some of his fellow officers drifted near. Apart from the S.S. officers they were mostly strangers to each other, and the blue-shirted lieutenant wasn't known to most.

They saw more objects taken from the pockets and thrown into the stream. Then someone realized what they were—keys such as one finds in hotels, with big brass plaques attached to them.

A whole handful of keys cascaded into the water. Then the morose-looking lieutenant rose. He looked at the surprised faces round him, said, 'What a bloody, stupid thing war is!' and walked away.

No one ever solved the mystery of the lieutenant with two

pocketsful of hotel keys.   Unless it was that more than the
L.R.D.G. had over-indulged the previous day.

They covered more than two hundred miles that first
day on their journey towards their unknown objective.   Two
hundred miles, and every one away from the front line beyond
Alexandria; two hundred miles that took them deeper
into the African continent.

In the late afternoon, the palm-lined Nile road took them
in towards a small Egyptian town called El Minya.   The
men understood that this was to be their halting-place for
the night.   They were glad of it—two hundred miles con-
fined to a bumping, bouncing truck was beginning to chafe
the restless spirits of the commando-trained men.

On the outskirts of the mud-dwellinged town a solitary
L.R.D.G. truck skulked in the shadow of a high mud wall;
when the driver saw the convoy, the truck started up,
jumped into speed and piloted them through the town.
The quarters, it transpired, were rather unusual.

They were led into a big yard fronting large, hangar-like
buildings.   It proved to be a cotton mill.   The commando
was told to bed down for the night on soft bales of cotton,
but first there was going to be a party.

Amid cheers, cartons of ice-cold canned beer were
brought across to the men, along with food that rarely
figured in the British Army's menu.   The officers went
along to a beautiful white house on the banks of the Nile
to meet the owner of the mill.   To the surprise of most of
them, the owner proved to be a lieutenant-colonel in the
British Intelligence Corps.   His name, when introduced,
was John Haselden.   It seemed that he was of that breed
of men who make their careers in foreign countries; for the
mills and house were his, and clearly he was a man of
wealth and standing.

He was a good host, a most friendly and likeable man.
Rather tall and strong-looking, his face was browned in a
manner which showed constant exposure to the sun.   But
what impressed the commando officers most was the effect

of Colonel Haselden's presence upon the local Arabs: when he walked by they prostrated themselves before him and tried to kiss his hand or the bottom of his bush-jacket. It reminded them of a feudal lord with his tenants, and yet Haselden was ever courteous and friendly, smiling upon the men who paid him such deep homage.

For the officers it was quite a magical party. They dined in the cool of the evening at long, white-naperied tables in a delightful garden alongside a swimming pool. Some charming ladies, friends of Colonel Haselden, were present, helping to enliven the party. Beyond the tall yew hedge of the garden flowed the magic Nile of history and legend.

An army of *suffragi* attended to the diners; almost it seemed as if each officer had his own personal attendant bringing one rich dish after another for his delectation, It was all very delightful, as was the midnight boating on the Nile afterwards to the strains of an Arab orchestra. It was with regret that finally they retired to their beds. All knew that the morning would see a change in their life— there would be no more parties, and no more boating. But all agreed that the commando had started well.

II

ANOTHER surprise awaited them in the morning. When their trucks rolled out of the mill yard, the smiling, friendly Colonel Haselden was there to wave them good-bye. It was puzzling, because in some curious way the men had concluded that he was something to do with their expedition, and yet he was remaining behind.

The commando stopped speculating, however, settled themselves as comfortably as possible on the piled-up gear in their trucks, and noted carefully the route their vehicles took, once outside El Minya. They saw they were still travelling south, putting more miles between them and the battlefront beyond Alexandria.

All morning they travelled, making good time on the mud track that wound with the curving of the slow-running Nile, until they came to Asyut. Then Captain Lloyd Owen in the leading patrol car swung off the track and headed away from the Nile. For the men it seemed as though at last their journey was just beginning.

The going became suddenly much worse. The trucks lurched and bounced in a way that threw the men about on top of kit which continually worked loose from its lashings and danced disconcertingly all over the metal floors of their Chev 3-tonners. It became suddenly grim, hard work for the commando, holding on and trying to anticipate the worst of the vehicles' pitchings.

Yet even now, as they were to realize in three days' time, the way was still comparatively good—in a few days they were to look back on the route to El Dakhla as if it were a joy-ride.

There was a track from Asyut across the desert to Dakhla Oasis, two hundred miles to the south-west. It was one of

the oldest tracks in the world, one that had been followed
by camel trains for thousands of years, but as the commando
heartily agreed, it was nothing to write home about.

A way beaten by many feet led a winding route among
the sandhills of a glaring, heat-ridden desert. Not always
was the way apparent, however; many times sand had
flooded across the track, so that it was lost to sight, and
they were dependent upon the navigators with the L.R.D.G.,
cruising always a quarter of a mile or so ahead. And
sometimes during those three days they had need of their
sand drill, to release trucks gripped by the soft, shifting
sand that swilled over their wheel rims and held them
immovable until sweating men dug sand channels under
spinning wheels.

It was hard going, the hardest part deriving from the
raging thirst that gripped them from morning till night.
For now the commando was on the L.R.D.G. desert ration
of water. Half a gallon per man per day, out of which
each had to make a contribution towards the daily topping-
up of radiators!

The men suffered stoically, but though a few were upset
physically by the long hours of jolting under the merciless
sun, mentally they kept in fine fettle. No one talked about
going back.

The one disturbing feature in the days of following the old
camel trail was the increasing sickness of the commando's
kilted leader, Major Colin Campbell. Shortly before they
reached Dakhla Oasis it became apparent that he had
contracted dysentery.

It was a relief when finally they saw the feather-headed
palms of the oasis late one afternoon across the undulating
sandy wastes. Spirits rose. The L.R.D.G. had told them
at one of the halts that Dakhla wasn't much of an oasis,
but at least there was unlimited fresh, cool water there. It
would have needed a tank corps to have kept the commando
away from the water that evening, and never had it tasted
so refreshing for most of them.

But there was no long rest for them. They were driving

to schedule, and long halts weren't yet on the programme.

Next morning the thirteen vehicles pulled south-west from Dakhla. It proved to be a nightmarish day for most of them. Now there was no track to follow, and the ground was broken and stony. Trucks, occupants and contents were given a most tremendous shaking-up. There were hills to hold down their speed, too, and when nightfall came after their hardest day since leaving Cairo, they had covered the shortest distance. Next day it grew a little better, though not much. They passed out of the hilly area and ran into sand again.

On this desert driving tactics changed. No longer did they drive in something of an orderly convoy. Rather, it took on the appearance of a wild cavalry charge, with every truck finding its own route and going flat out across the sandy wastes. The object of the manœuvre was to keep moving at all costs. As soon as momentum was lost their vehicles became bogged down in the soft sand and had to be dug out. That was a job no one liked in that awful heat.

Clouds of dust were thrown up as the vehicles raced madly along; the powdery, bitter fog swirled about the men in the vehicles and covered them with a clinging yellow-grey dust that blocked their nostrils, built up in ridges around sweat marks, dusted their eyebrows and eyelashes, and made them look like ghastly apparitions. It got everywhere, so that dry mouths were unpleasantly gritty, and eyes stung to the lash of driving particles.

Even the drivers of the trucks were little better off. True they had shade from their cab roofs, but the dust swirled over them, too, because all glass had been removed from the vehicles.

If a truck became embedded in the sand, no one halted to help it out—for that would have meant two trucks stuck and not just one. It was up to the occupants of each truck to work out its own salvation, and sweating and cursing as they dug, losing skin off their shoulders as they heaved to get the 3-tonners moving again, they somehow fought their way through the bad patches.

The L.R.D.G. were rarely bogged down. They were experts at keeping their vehicles moving.

Every hour or so, Lloyd Owen would find a patch of firm ground and halt while the stragglers came in. It was clear that the L.R.D.G. were not altogether liking their rôle of shepherd to such big and clumsy sheep. Grudgingly they recognized that it was no fault of the commando, who worked like Trojans to keep up the pace, but a brooding L.R.D.G., no less sensitive to the sun, must have kept thinking that without the 3-tonners they could have cut days off their schedule. The desert was enough to make even hardened L.R.D.G. men short-tempered and irritable.

One thing, however, was that by now everyone knew their immediate destination—it could only be Kufra, magic oasis on the edge of the Great Sand Sea, five hundred miles south of the Mediterranean coastline. Their immediate destination; but where they would go from there only a few officers, including Lloyd Owen, knew. The men couldn't have cared less, anyway. During the day they sweated and cursed as they fought to keep the vehicles moving, with no thoughts beyond their next halt and a chance to rest and wet their dry, aching throats. At night, though, with the cool shadows of evening, when the desert is the loveliest place on earth, they would relax and seem to expand. And then, fit, healthy young men, their resolution came back and they found they had enjoyed the hardships of the trail in some curious way, so that when morning came they rolled willingly out of their dusty blankets and prepared for another assault on the hostile, sun-drenched desert land.

There were few points of interest on their journey. Once they were guided to a cliff face by the L.R.D.G., who with the modest pride of ownership that went beyond time and nationalism showed the suitably impressed commando a cave upon whose walls was a writing by some prehistoric cave-dweller. More prosaically, the L.R.D.G. used the place as a dump, and there was a drum of petrol there.

On another day they saw what everyone declared to be a mountain. It was a bald, red, sandstone ridge that jutted

abruptly from the desert, towering above them. The
L.R.D.G. told them that this was the celebrated Gilf Kebir,
a notable landmark in an area not noted for topographical
features. It marked the southerly limit of the Great Sand
Sea, that treacherous, apparently impassable sand barrier,
greater in extent than all Ireland. It was this Sand Sea
which put a restriction on direct movement in the desert,
and virtually was the *raison d'être* for the L.R.D.G. It
meant that they had rounded the mass, and could now go
quickly on towards Kufra.

Eight days out from Cairo they struck a caravan trail that
linked Kufra with Wadi Halfa and Khartoum. Spirits
rose. Ahead of them stretched a wonderful golden flatness,
upon which their trucks sped as if traversing the finest
concrete highway. There was an exhilaration about their
passage across the yellow sand; it was like driving through
soft snow, with all sounds curiously muted, their engines
purring in a way that was soporific, almost sleep-inducing.

The peace of that wonderful afternoon was suddenly
shattered by a sharp, warning cry. Everyone looked up.
They saw agitation on the part of the L.R.D.G. Lloyd
Owen was signalling from his penanted vehicle. The
startled commando saw the six lighter vehicles roaring
away from them, turning in a big crescent behind their
leader, engines screaming under the frenzied demands for
acceleration.

Someone in the commando party was pointing north-east.
A rolling cloud of dust could be seen on the horizon. Dust.
That could only mean the passage of other vehicles. The
officers in the commando remembered what Lloyd Owen
had told them, coming up. He wasn't expecting to encounter any other L.R.D.G. convoy. But here something
moved on wheels, and if it was not the restless, always mobile
L.R.D.G., whom could it be but the enemy?

The officers in charge of each truck remembered the drill
they had rehearsed on their second day out in the desert.
In case of a meeting with the enemy, the 3-tonners would
keep going away from the threat; the L.R.D.G. would go

in to tackle the enemy and try to hold them off while the commando escaped.

The trucks roared on towards near-by Kufra. All eyes watched the swirling dust clouds from Lloyd Owen's receding vehicles. They saw the L.R.D.G. go circling in towards a now-revealed column of vehicles. They looked like suspicious dogs in the distance, feeling out a possible adversary. Then the L.R.D.G. came racing back to the commando.

It was a friendly column, they were told. It was a force of S.A.S. (Special Air Service), also moving in to Kufra on an expedition of their own. They were well behind schedule and in theory should have been out of the area, hence the suspicions of the L.R.D.G. All of which was relieving to know.

The two forces joined and bowled merrily along the last distance into Kufra. When they reached it the milometers said they had covered 997 miles since leaving Cairo.

III

KUFRA astonished the commando unit; they had expected the usual, comparatively small oasis. But this stretched as far as the eye could see, being, in parts, fifty miles wide.

The oasis was in a depression, considerably below sea level, and the trains of vehicles had a fine view across Kufra as they descended from the smooth going of the past hours. They saw scattered palms, still and graceful in the dying rays of the sun, green cultivated strips everywhere telling of good water, and several Arab towns or villages. The green looked particularly welcome to their desert-jaded eyes, and they swept into Kufra exultantly.

Near to where they were halted for the night, under the date palms, they were surprised to see an airstrip. They had not realized that our forces were so well organized so deep into the desert. One or two Bombays were at one end of the field, readying for a take-off, and they could see a considerable number of sheds like workshops in amongst the trees. Evidently the L.R.D.G. were using Kufra as a forward base for their operations, and they had equipped themselves well. At one time they had had a number of even more advanced bases, including Siwa and Jalo Oases, but with the big retreat down the coast to Alamein, they had been obliged to desert these posts to save their being cut off by a victory-flushed enemy.

The men were told they would be six days resting in Kufra, and they were encouraged to make the most of it in order to be fit again for another, possibly even more hazardous journey. They didn't need telling twice.

There was a glorious period of relaxation under the shadowy palms, just letting the weariness flow out of tired

bones. Then, seeming to get their strength back in magic-
ally short time, they began to take an interest in their
surroundings. They learned that there were two swimming-
pools in the vicinity. One was a tin-lined affair made by
the L.R.D.G., muddy-bottomed but fresh and cool to
their bodies; the other was a salt lake, as intensely salty
as the Dead Sea, and just as painful to men with desert
sores and sweat rashes.

Some of the men plaited lean-to shelters to protect themselves from the sun during the heat of the day. Those not
caring for such elaborations, took siesta just as they slept
at nights, under a palm tree, moving round with the shadow
as the Arabs did. The tree-lovers would awaken in the
morning to find their one blanket sticky with dates that had
fallen in the night.

A few parades were held, but they were inconsiderable
affairs after which, kit and other duties attended to, the
troops were pretty much free to laze around or find means
of enjoyment. This meant for most an occasional stroll
round the nearest Arab township and a spot of haggling
over fruit or eggs in the crowded market square. However,
Kufra villages seemed much like any others along
the Sweet Water Canal, and persistent flies soon deterred
them and sent them to the clean, breezy edge of the desert
again.

On a hill inside the oasis was a massive Italian-built
fortress. Until the nineteen-thirties Kufra had been a place
of legend to Infidels, with only a few white explorers ever
having set foot in the place. Then Mussolini decided it
would be a brave thing to capture this peaceful desert
civilization, and he sent troops in such numbers and with
such modern weapons of war that Kufra had no chance
against his army. A fortress was built—chiefly by unwilling
Arab labour—and the flag of the conqueror unfurled from
its flagstaff. Ten years later a French force under General
Leclerc routed the Italian garrison and Kufra had been
held as a base for the Desert Army ever since. The change
was welcomed by the local Arabs, who everywhere in Libya

hated the cruel, oppressive Italians, and for that reason were staunch friends of the Allied Forces.

To this fortress went some of the commando officers in search of more petrol for their vehicles. They found it occupied by the Sudan Defence Force, with also a company of the Welch Regiment—a curious place in which to discover the accents of Swansea and Cardiff.

Here they heard more rumours, confirming the talk that was being whispered all around the oasis. It seemed that several expeditions were being planned to operate simultaneously from Kufra. The S.A.S., whom they had joined on the way in to Kufra, were to attack Benghazi, the object being the destruction of shipping in the harbour, port facilities and anything else they could wreck in a swift foray that would occupy only a few hours of one dark, moonless night. It was a sharp, hit-and-run raid against far superior forces, but with a calculated possibility of success because of the surprise element behind the attack.

Another party, consisting of Sudan Defence Force, was to go out and try to recapture the fort at Jalo, a vital place on the routes between Kufra and Benghazi, Tobruk and Barce.

A third raid was to be by the L.R.D.G., to attempt the destruction of aircraft on the airfield at Barce.

And their own mixed commando force? What was to be their target? By now the men were having guesses—good ones, too.

One good thing about the halt at Kufra was that members of the party got to know each other better. The S.S. commandos were strangers to the attached personnel, and on the way in from Cairo there had been little opportunity for social encounter. The men, including the officers with each vehicle, had lived and messed together as truck units, and fatigue of the day had largely kept them from visiting each other's fires on an evening on the long desert trek.

But relaxing in the oasis at Kufra made for social intercourse, and in time personalities emerged. At this time there were thirteen officers in the party.

The O.C., Major Colin Campbell, proud to wear the Hodden Grey of the London Scottish, was rather older than most of his officers and men.   He was a keen disciplinarian, a man for whom others found words such as 'unswerving', 'iron-willed', and 'indomitable' to describe him.   One member of his party at least thought him the finest, bravest gentleman he had ever met.   Campbell was to demonstrate all these qualities in the next weeks.

Second-in-command was Lieutenant Graham Taylor. He was probably the ideal type of commando officer, forceful, aggressive, and quite heedless of danger in time of action.   Perhaps he had too little patience; perhaps in attack he was over-impetuous.   And he was intolerant of attempts to introduce parade-ground discipline into desert warfare.   But he was an excellent type for commando work.

Graham Taylor, months before, had received training with the masters of desert warfare, a New Zealand section of the L.R.D.G.   His experience had proved invaluable in the preparations for this desert journey.

Taylor's usual companion was Lieutenant Michael Duffy, who had joined the S.S. from the Hampshire Regiment.   A Scot claiming Glasgow for a home town, Duffy had also seen action with the L.R.D.G., and was a desert-wise warrior. He was popular, perhaps because he didn't give a damn what people thought about him.   Neither did he give a damn for authority higher than himself.   He was a most resolute, independent officer.

Two Royal Northumberland Fusiliers officers were in the party, too.   They were the machine-gun experts of the commando.   One was Lieutenant Ronald Murphy, inevitably, if unoriginally, Spud to his companions.   He was a rather short, literary type who yet seemed to enjoy commando work.   Even on the arduous trek, though, he seemed to find time to curl up in any shade with a book.

Lieutenant Mike Roberts, R.N.F., was a big, hearty fellow, with a laugh that seemed to ring throughout the camp. He was the M.T. expert, and the fine performance of the Chevs on the desert journey was a credit to the M.T. Officer.

Third-in-command was Lieutenant Hugh Davidson Sillito. He was an Argyll, another warrior whose kilt brightened the K.D. drabness of the desert commando. David Sillito was a man of charm, a man seemingly utterly without fear. To those who knew him he appeared to be recklessly brave, yet there were depths to Sillito—he was a man of intelligence who had more in his mind than he let the world see.

A second-lieutenant was with the S.S. He was a New Zealander, Bill MacDonald. Mac was a character. He was a wanderer and soldier of fortune who had fought Franco in Spain and seen most countries of the world. He was boldly courageous in action, though a little uneasy yet because of the newness of his solitary pip. The one thing that riled the New Zealander was to be called a 'colonial'. Disgust would last for days against the offender.

These seven were S.S. officers; attached were six others. Biggest was Lieutenant Tom Langton, an Irish Guards officer, now in the Special Boat Service. Langton, an ex-rowing Blue, was a man fated to be in on rather crazy expeditions. A recent harrowing one had demanded that he should hang on to the stern rail of a speeding M.T.B. and lob sticky limpet mines against enemy supply barges. It had been a trying experience because the limpets would insist on sticking to Lieutenant Langton just when he was about to hurl them away. Because he had no special duties during the desert journey, Langton had become adjutant to the commando. Very quickly he became a most popular officer with the men, who competed to get into his party.

George Harrison, a Northerner, was an R.E. lieutenant attached to the commando. With him were eight sappers and masses of explosives. Harrison was a quiet, fair-haired, rather tall man and, like Murphy, rather retiring in himself. A friendly, likeable personality, the other officers soon found, and with a courage that was to manifest itself later.

The Royal Corps of Signals was represented by Lieutenant M. H. Trollope, reputed to be a descendant of the distinguished author of that name. 'Trolly' to everyone, he quickly became quite a character in the party. For one thing, he seemed so out of place in a desert commando. He hated the desert, wilted in the sun, and seemed not at all a fighting man, yet he had volunteered for the expedition. He would cheerfully say that he didn't know what he was doing with the commando, but he never complained and was an asset to morale all during the time they were together. The most characteristic sight at halts was Trolly wearing a wide-brimmed hat, trying to find some place out of the sun.

Two R.A. officers were on the expedition. John Poynton was a Coast Defence gunner lieutenant who had four men with him. Poynton was nursing an arm that had been broken in Cyprus a few weeks earlier—he had kept hidden the fact that he was now medically down-graded because of the arm, in case he was hauled out of the commando. Again, he was rather older than the other lieutenants, and in fact was usually referred to as 'Old John'. But he was a nimble old 'un, well able to hold his own with everyone. Again he was a man who seemed insensible to danger, and completely nerveless in times of crisis.

The other artillery subaltern was Hugh R. Barlow. Bill —he hated the name Hugh—quickly became an outstanding personality in the party. He was a big fellow, whom even his most loyal friends could only describe as 'rugged' in appearance. There have been Barlows in every age, and always they have been doing something bold and adventurous—pirating, starting revolutions or finding ways across unexplored continents. That, at least, was how his new companions regarded him.

Barlow loved the desert and, unlike Trollope, luxuriated in the heat. Outside the L.R.D.G. he was probably the most desert-experienced man in the commando. He had been in the siege of Tobruk and for over two years fought up and down the desert in most of the campaigns. He seemed mostly in his element when he was in the midst of a fight. Quite a man, Bill Barlow.

He was, incidentally, the only officer to wear the

washed out blue shirt most commonly associated with Indian or New Zealand troops.

They had a doctor in the party. He was a black-moustached six-footer, Captain John Gibson, R.A.M.C. Gibby was a Canadian, a cool customer when it came to action, and later was to prove himself a man of resource and very great spirit. He had a nice dry sense of humour, and an unusualness about his treatment of ills that was to become a source of conversation among the commando.

A squadron sergeant-major from the Leicesters was with the expedition. He was the biggest man in the commando; a rather grim, purposeful man named Swinburn. He was a disciplinarian who plainly was not happy at first at the casual camaraderie between the unshaven commando officers and men, but in time he seemed to accept things and became very popular all round.

Swinburn was another cool customer, reacting with calmness to any tight situations; his strength was loyalty —to his officers and men, and to his beloved Leicestershire Regiment. It was Swinburn who thought that Major Campbell was the finest officer he had ever had the honour to serve under.

Yet even the seeming stiff-backed, rigid disciplinarian of a sergeant-major had his softer side, his men were to discover. He held a modest fancy for himself—as a trombonist.

Five sergeants were in the commando. Sergeant Evans, tall, slim, a regular from the Welsh Guards; Sergeant Jock Walsh, Black Watch, quietly capable; Sergeant Paddy O'Neill, quick, tenacious, Tipperary's contribution to the war effort; and then an Englishman from the West Country, the Armourer, Sergeant Alford, R.A.O.C. The fifth was a Paignton man, Sergeant Hore.

And the men—too many to be listed. Privates Cusick, Mackintosh, Green, Hancock, Pugh and Powell. Hogan of the Irish Guards. Two London Scots named Allardyce and MacKay, the former of international rugby standard.

Wimpey Glynn, Nobby Mills, Corporal Beale, and Ted Ashford, who looked like Clark Gable but was a whole lot tougher.

All were men of character, men who had fretted against disciplined Army life and had volunteered for less formal if infinitely more hazardous commando operations. They were a rough bunch, bad boys around a base camp, but the right stuff for this desert commando.

Campbell must have felt that he had dependable men with him even if they did make the sergeant-major wince at their easy interpretation of Army discipline.

IV

Six days as a period of rest from desert travel sounded fine at first, but after two or three days a curious impatience took hold of the men. They began to feel faintly restless; perhaps they were tiring of being kept in the dark, while all other troops in the oasis seemed to know their destination.

But they had to curb their impatience; certainly the suffering, dysentery-afflicted but still soldierly Major Campbell was not divulging any secrets yet. In time they would be told. Meanwhile they must attend to their minor fatigues and rest up for the days ahead.

They began to have a feeling that they were waiting for something—either that or they were waiting for someone. On their fourth day in Kufra they realized it was the latter.

That day, within hours of each other, Bombay transport planes flew laboriously in to the Kufra airstrip. The first —which had come from Cairo via Wadi Halfa in the Sudan—brought two additional officers to the party, and four German-born recruits. The other brought them an R.A.F. flying officer, and the man who had originated the idea behind the commando.

It was all very surprising for the commando. They sat up under the shady palm trees as the first arrivals came in off the airstrip. Their astonished eyes saw two British officers—one a captain, the other a lieutenant—shepherding four German-uniformed, German-armed men into their camp. They continued to be surprised when the captain took the Germans a little distance away and almost immediately upon their arrival began to drill them. The drill was German, and the commands were German, too. It sounded somehow unreal, to hear the harsh German orders ringing out in the midst of a British encampment, and some of the men never felt easy about the situation and always afterwards regarded the German party with mild distrust.

The commando officers soon learned the identity of the newcomers. They were S.I.G. men, yet another of the astonishing irregular units which flourished during the desert campaigns.

The S.I.G.—Special Indentification Group—was something in the order of a suicide squad. Their work demanded a degree of daring which inevitably meant ultimate detection by the enemy, and detection was, for most of them, something rather worse than death.

For most of the S.I.G. were Jews born in Germany; their war-time work was to operate in most brazen manner behind the enemy lines disguised as Germans. When they were captured death was considered too good for them. They were regarded by Germans as traitors fighting against their Fatherland, and in addition they were Jews. Generally they were tortured, and in preference to being captured alive, S.I.G. men would kill themselves when plans went awry.

The S.I.G. numbered twenty-one at full strength. It had two officers, Captain Herbert Bray and Lieutenant David Lanark both officers were to accompany the commando—both were remarkable men.

Captain Bray had seen service up the desert with the celebrated 4th Indian Division until being placed in charge of the S.I.G. He was a brilliant scholar at Oxford, an incomparable linguist, a good musician and poet of no mean ability. He spoke several Indian dialects, and was fluent in German.

Herbert Bray was a man so far gifted mentally that it made him aloof from his fellows: there were some who felt uneasy in his presence, even far higher-ranking officers. And yet the few who were his intimates could accept his sometimes curious, rather chilly manner, and joke with him about it.

He had a restless, questing mind, and he was forever planning, and planning brilliantly. His plans seemed fantastic to many, yet his men trusted them because they always seemed to come off. He seemed completely without fear, and his men would follow him anywhere.

Lieutenant Lanark, a Scots Guards officer, was another brilliant linguist, reputed to be fluent in six German dialects. He too was fearless, and yet with it all, unlike the sometimes impulsive Bray, there was much caution in him. Lanark was inclined to trust no one, while Bray, according to his men, trusted some too much. When Lanark made plans it was very coolly, most calculatedly done, but once made he would see them through to the end. Only when he was driving was Lanark reckless. Then he liked to have the speedometer as near to the eighty mark as possible, and his followers inevitably dubbed him 'The Flying Scotsman'.

The four 'Germans' were a plump, cheerful little corporal named Steiner, and three privates, Wilenski, Berg and Weizmann. All were very young, about nineteen at the time.

Weizmann's story was typical of his companions'. It was the story of a political madman's rise to power, with the use of anti-Semiticism to bolster a Nazi régime. Weizmann's father had disappeared into a concentration camp in the nineteen-thirties, where he died in the manner that millions were to die. Young Weizmann, sixteen at the time, was hastily sent to Palestine, where he was living in 1939 when war broke out in Europe.

A boy with a memory, he instantly volunteered into British service. When he found that this meant he would be restricted to some administrative branch of the service in Palestine, Weizmann promptly hitch-hiked to Egypt to volunteer for more active service. Three times he broke camp, and three times he was brought back to face charges. Then someone in Cairo said, 'This is the kind of chap we are looking for,' and Weizmann's problems were over . . . or just beginning.

Some of the commando had heard of the S.I.G., but little

was known by the Desert Army of their work at the time. Much more, in fact, was known to the enemy, who were seeking the S.I.G. with most ferocious ideas regarding the German-born Jews should they fall into their hands. The enemy knew of the S.I.G.'s existence because out of their twenty-one members two had been traitors.

The Palestinians—for they had renounced their German nationality years before—mixed a little with the rest of the commando, and in fact later travelled dispersed among the trucks when the trek was resumed. But all the same their two officers kept the German group much to themselves. They did not want their men 'contaminated' by British soldierly ways, by drills and even a bearing which was un-Germanic. S.I.G. men were not expected to live long, anyway, and it was the little things that gave them away to the enemy.

Bray and Lanark were sticklers for detail. Their four Palestinians always wore real German issue uniforms, even to their underwear and socks; any cigarettes or chocolates they carried had to be German; and they were not allowed to speak to their officers except in the German tongue. When they marched it was in the German way, with hands swinging across the body—a salute had to be German . . . they, in fact, had to think and feel that they were Germans.

They were an audacious little group. They had tried themselves out on the enemy some months earlier near Bardia. They had sneaked through the enemy lines in German-marked vehicles, then boldly set a barrier across the road and stopped all traffic on it. In the guise of German military police they had questioned drivers and made notes of troops and vehicles passing through the area. A bold beginning, with some very valuable information for British Intelligence upon the return.

Other forays had followed. The S.I.G. used to wander behind the enemy lines, occasionally creating acts of sabotage but more often merely keeping their eyes open and returning with vital information regarding enemy troop movements. They would pull in at German canteens and buy their cigarettes or chocolates, while Bray and Lanark calmly entered enemy officers' messes and discussed the war situation there.

When traitors tipped off the Germans about the operations of the S.I.G., a close watch was kept for the intruders by the enemy. Once, because of it, Bray and Lanark were detected in a mess attached to a panzer corps, and they had to shoot their way out of it.

The traitors (depending what is meant by traitors) were two Germans named Esser and Brückner, P.O.W.s in Egypt, who offered to work for the Allies, saying they were fanatically anti-Nazi. They were not Jews. Both had served in the French Foreign Legion before rejoining the German army. Because of their recent Afrika Korps' experience, they were welcomed and put to training the S.I.G. in the latest German drills. The Palestinians mistrusted them from the start, and so did Lanark, but Captain Bray was more trusting and accepted them in good faith.

One night German-dressed S.I.G.s ferried some Free French troops behind the enemy lines on a sabotage operation to Martuba airfield. Captain Bray took a party to Derna to destroy aircraft there, the same night. Of the Martuba expedition, only the French lieutenant in charge came back.

He said that suddenly, in the darkness, the truck halted. The driver—Brückner—was heard to say, 'Something's fallen off the truck. I'm going back for it.'

Brückner climbed out of the cab and went off into the night. Minutes passed. Suddenly the lieutenant became alert. He heard two Palestinian S.I.G.s speaking inside the cab. One was saying, 'Brückner is away a long time.'

The other said, 'I'm uneasy. I don't trust Brückner. I think he might play traitor.'

Then dark forms began to materialize out of the blackness. A German command rang out. Fire stabbed in the night and lead came spinning into the crowded truck. Men screamed in agony, while others fell out of the truck and began frantically to reply to the fire.

There seemed no way of escape, and yet somehow the French lieutenant blundered through the encircling enemy. He reported seeing the two Palestinians hurling grenades with reckless abandon at the advancing enemy. Then, when they were on the point of capture, they each drew the pin from a grenade and held it to them. Afterwards British Intelligence learned that Martuba airfield had had advance information about the raid.

Brückner was flown back to Berlin where he was fêted and awarded, according to some, the *Deutsche Kreuze in Gold*, which is two grades higher than the Iron Cross, 1st Class. In Egypt, Esser was suddenly found to have contacts with a Cairo fifth column and arrested. He was shot by the S.I.G. —while trying to escape, they reported.

Not much of this story was known to the commando at the time; it came out a long while afterwards. All the commando knew was that two very brisk, very efficient officers had joined them, along with four men, to all intents and purposes German soldiers. The commando spent their time puzzling over the matter, wondering how S.I.G. fitted into the plans that were still not known to most of them.

That day, two days before the commando took the trail again, seemed to drag. Perhaps the men were beginning to fret against the inactivity, or were finding too little to do.

Lieutenant Roberts was down in the M.T. lines, supervising the maintenance of their gallant vehicles; with him was Murphy. Trolly was trying to find some shade and was resisting an invitation to join Graham Taylor and Mike Duffy on one of their social visits to old friends in the Benghazi party of S.A.S. Major Campbell was lying down, exhausted. Black-moustached Captain Gibson was speaking to him, urging some course. Campbell, eyes closed, kept shaking his head. Nearly everyone else was trekking towards the swimming-pool.

When the next Bombay landed there were few of the commando around to witness its arrival. But Captain Lloyd Owen was out in the sunshine to greet it; they saw him returning after a while, walking slowly with a man of higher rank, a man carrying a briefcase.

When the commando returned for their evening meal, they were astonished to find they had a new C.O. Major Campbell had, after all, been second-in-command. And the feeling of intrigue deepened when they recognized the pleasant, smiling newcomer with the briefcase.

It was their host at the El Minya cotton mill, Lieutenant-Colonel John Haselden.

With the arrival of John Haselden at Kufra the vague sense of frustration and waiting departed. Now everyone realized what they had been waiting for—their leader, the inspirer, as they were to learn, of the whole project. They looked at the briefcase, rarely out of Haselden's hand, and waited for the secret of the destination to be divulged.

Next day they paraded. Major Campbell handed over to Colonel Haselden, who stepped forward to look over his men. They were an unshaven, cut-throat looking lot in that early morning sunshine, but they must have seemed ripe material for the project in hand.

Haselden said, smiling as he nearly always was: 'Sit down, gentlemen.' And when they were down on the sand—'I know you are anxious to learn of your destination, and what work has been planned for this commando. Now I am going to let you into the picture.'

He paused. The men waited, silent, rather tense. Slowly he began to spread a large map before them. When Haselden spoke again it was to say something incredible.

'Gentlemen, we are going to capture Tobruk and destroy it.'

V

Just like that. They were going to wrest Tobruk from the enemy and destroy it. The men looked at each other. Even including the R.A.F. pilot, Pilot-Officer A. L. Scott, who had attached himself to the commando with Haselden the previous afternoon, and the German party, their strength totalled only eighty-one. Eighty-one to capture a fortress which had defied the Axis' armies for months, even though it had capitulated with surprising suddenness to Rommel little more than three months earlier.

Colonel Haselden laughed, understanding what was flowing through their minds. He was a solid, brown-faced, rather homely-looking officer, in some curious way inspiring to his new troops.

Haselden let the murmuring die down, then he said, 'The idea sounds fantastic, but it would also sound fantastic to the enemy, and it is for that very reason we are going to do just what I have just said—take Tobruk from the enemy, hold it for twelve hours and leave it so that afterwards it is useless as a supply port for the Afrika Korps.'

At the first meeting he did not give all the details to the commando, but he revealed sufficient to make the men feel that the idea was not quite as hare-brained as it had first sounded.

'We are going to drive openly into Tobruk one evening just at dusk. We will enter as prisoners-of-war captured at the Alamein front, under the guard of German soldiers.'— That explained the S.I.G.—'We are going to capture a bridgehead just outside Tobruk harbour itself, under cover of the biggest air raid this coast has ever seen.'

And liaison with the R.A.F. would explain the presence of Pilot-Officer Scott.

35

'Because we will not be expected, we shall establish a bridgehead without difficulty. Then, through this little harbour we have captured, M.T.B.s will pour in reinforcements.'

Now the naval ratings were explained. More liaison, this time with the Royal Navy.

Haselden went on talking. One thing was certain, he had no doubts about the scheme himself; he simply would not admit the possibility of the plan going awry, and his confidence quickly transmitted itself to his men so that they, too, believed in it.

'Argyll and Sutherland Highlanders will be landed off M.T.B.s. With them will be a platoon of Royal Northumberland Fusiliers—a machine-gun regiment.' Better names could not have been quoted for an assault party— the Argylls who had fought throughout the desert campaigns, and the R.N.F. who had been in every bitter battle too.

The M.T.B. party was to be called Force C; their own party Force B.

'When Force C has landed we are going to break out from our bridgehead and fight our way along the south side of Tobruk harbour, then hold the west flank against any reinforcements which might come in from the desert. Even so, our force, like the R.A.F., will be largely diversionary. While we command the enemy's attention on the south shore, two destroyers will come quietly in north of Tobruk harbour and land a much larger force of marines. They will smash their way through Tobruk town itself and will link up with us at a place near to the Italian hospital.'

Haselden paused again, watching for the reaction of his audience. But the scrub-chinned, sun-blackened faces betrayed little of what they were thinking.

'We are going to hold off the enemy during a night and a morning. During that time our demolition squads will destroy piers and dock installations; our M.T.B.s and destroyers will enter the harbour and sink all shipping where it will most inconvenience the enemy afterwards. There is a tank repair workshop north of the harbour—the marines will render that useless to the enemy. West of the town is the most vital target of all—Rommel's bomb-proof oil-storage tanks. *We* are going to destroy that.'

Oil, tanks, shipping. The three things Rommel must have to continue his fight in Africa. Destroy his shipping and Tobruk harbour in the process; with Tobruk useless he would have to depend on Benghazi, and that would add over two hundred miles to his supply routes. Then they remembered that Colonel Stirling's S.A.S. were not far away in Kufra at that moment, with intentions to do no good to Benghazi.

Destroy Rommel's tank repair shop—burn the fuel upon which his army ran. The men began to realize the implication of what Colonel Haselden was saying. Suddenly they realized that they had been selected to deal the enemy a damaging blow, one which might virtually knock him out of the African continent altogether. For they knew that British and Dominion reinforcements were being poured into Egypt, and they were too good soldiers not to know that very soon a re-equipped Allied army would smash its way into Cyrenaica and beyond again. And they could help the forthcoming battle; they could pave the way by crippling Rommel's supply port.

Haselden was saying, 'For twelve hours we will hold out. There will be no retreat. Twelve hours is all the time the sappers need to do their work of demolition.'

A voice came from the ranks. 'Afterwards . . .? Do we come out through the desert?' Because everyone there realized the impossibility of such an attempt.

Haselden shook his head. 'The Navy will be there. You will be taken off in a destroyer.'

There was a mild cheer from some of the men.

'First-class passage to Alex!'

'That's better than desert travel!'

The plan was suddenly accepted completely and without reservation by the men. To them it seemed good enough. All the ends tied in nicely, they thought. And the more they considered it, the more their reckless spirits liked it. They couldn't see what could go wrong with the project. As their colonel said, surprise was on their side. Audacity would see them through. The last thing the enemy would expect to find would be a commando attacking Tobruk from the desert.

Next day there were active preparations for departure. But there was also another talk by the friendly-looking colonel with the briefcase, the mill owner from the Nile who had so surprisingly flown in to take charge of the expedition. Now Colonel Haselden was giving the commando details of the attack.

'Rommel has stripped Tobruk of its defences,' he told them, quoting Intelligence reports. 'All that remains to guard the port are a couple of battalions of third-rate Italian troops, plus a number of German technicians and ack-ack personnel. The German troops are not expected to total more than about one thousand.'

This was interesting news to the men. Low-grade Italian troops weren't an opposition to be feared by commandos; as for the German ack-ack they would presumably be occupied by the R.A.F., and technicians hardly rated as troops, even when German. Decidedly, they felt, the more they learned of this plan, the better it seemed to be.

Colonel Haselden took more maps from his briefcase and spread them where they could be studied by the men. Most of them had been in Tobruk, and the country was therefore familiar to them.

He showed them a cross marked on the map about twenty kilometres along the Tobruk to Bardia road. 'That's the danger point to our calculations. The Germans have a staging camp hereabouts, through which pass reinforcements brought by air from Europe. These are crack Panzer troops, intended to reinforce the Alamein front, and they are to be feared. They are the reason why we must fight our way to the west of the town and hold a line that covers the Bardia road.'

Then he showed them a name on the map that was unfamiliar to most of them: Mersa umm esc Sciausc. It

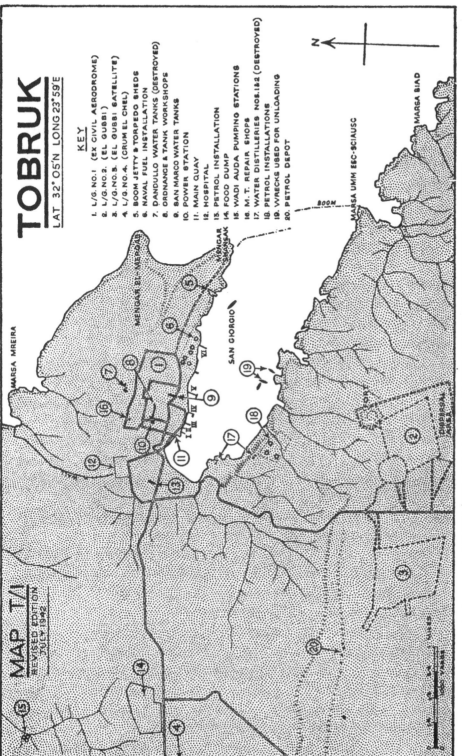

TOBRUK

LAT 32°05'N LONG 23°59'E

KEY

1. L/G. NO.1 (EX CIVIL AERODROME)
2. L/G. NO.2. (EL GUBBI)
3. L/G. NO.3. (EL GUBBI SATELLITE)
4. L/G. NO.4. (CRUM EL CHEL)
5. BOOM JETTY & TORPEDO SHEDS
6. NAVAL FUEL INSTALLATION
7. DANDULLO WATER TANKS (DESTROYED)
8. ORDNANCE & TANK WORKSHOPS
9. SAN MARCO WATER TANKS
10. POWER STATION
11. MAIN QUAY
12. HOSPITAL
13. PETROL INSTALLATION
14. FOOD DUMP
15. WADI AUDA PUMPING STATIONS
16. M.T. REPAIR SHOPS
17. WATER DISTILLERIES NOS.1&2 (DESTROYED)
18. PETROL INSTALLATIONS
19. WRECKS USED FOR UNLOADING
20. PETROL DEPOT

MAP T/1
REVISED EDITION
JULY 1942

MARSA MREIRA

MENGAR EL MERDUM

MARSA UMM ESC-SCIAUSC

MARSA BIAD

BOOM

SAN GIORGIO

TOBRUK—FROM THE SECRET MAP ISSUED TO THE FORCES OF OPERATION AGREEMENT

was the name of a tiny bay immediately outside the boom
net defences of Tobruk harbour, on the south side of the
port.

'This is the bay we are going to capture on September 13,'
Haselden's quiet, confident voice told them. 'Aerial reconnaissance photographs show coast defence guns mounted
around the cove, as well as ack-ack guns farther inland. Our
job is to capture those guns. If we fail, the Argylls and
R.N.F. will be blown out of the water when they come in to
land. But we will not fail. Then the coast defence guns
will be turned against the enemy. No enemy shipping
will be permitted to slip out of the harbour.'

There were more details. They were told the password
to the challenge, 'Who goes there?' It was, 'George
Robey.' Then the usual, 'Any questions?' Lieutenant
Poynton, the Coast Defence gunner, had one but kept it
until an officers' conference, later.

'I have only four gunners with me, sir. I cannot man a
battery of coast defence guns with that number.' He told
the colonel that originally it had been planned to bring
twenty-six gunners with him; twenty-two gunners had
been pulled out by higher planning somewhere, and in theory
were coming in by sea. But until then he would be unable
to man the coast guns. It was perturbing; it brought a frown
to Haselden's face.

Then the matter was forgotten as the commando began
preparations for the move-out the following morning.

Preparations. Once more examining, cleaning and oiling
their assorted guns; testing equipment and scrupulously,
carefully attending to the maintenance of their over-
burdened, sorely tried Chevrolets.

Captain Bray, with his S.I.G. followers, went down to
the M.T. lines to see Mike Roberts, following Colonel
Haselden's second talk. Bray was carrying some captured
enemy stencils, and Corporal Steiner brought paints and
brushes which had accompanied the S.I.G. on their bumpy,
monotonous trip from Cairo via Wadi Halfa.

Later the commando was surprised to see what had

happened to their vehicles. The British markings had been painted out, and now each door-panel bore the sign of the Afrika Korps—a palm tree behind a swastika. Across the bonnet of each Chev, too, was the sign of the *Beutezeichen* (sign of booty)—a foot wide stripe which the Germans painted on vehicles captured from the Allies. (At this time, Rommel's army pretty well functioned on captured trucks, food and oil obtained at the fall of Tobruk and during the precipitate retreat back to Alamein.) A divisional sign was also added—ER 372. This was the sign of a division which did exist and which in fact was stationed near Alamein. The S.I.G.'s Intelligence was very good and remarkably up to date.

When at last there was just nothing more that could be done to transport, arms or equipment, the commando gathered round their cooking fires, made a specially good supper, drank their rum and prepared to spend their last night in Kufra on terms favourable to themselves.

The L.R.D.G. were invited to join them. The L.R.D.G. had lost most of their aloofness now, and were inclined to be more tolerant towards the commando who had after all acquitted themselves well on the journey in to Kufra. Minor friendships were springing up between the two parties, and on this last night they sat and talked benevolently, reminiscing and exchanging information.

It seemed that after all the L.R.D.G. had more to do than just act as Cook's tourist guides to the expedition. They had to enter Tobruk perimeter, too, following some hours after the main commando. There was a radio-direction-finding station within the perimeter which G.H.Q., Cairo, wished to have destroyed, but not until Lloyd Owen had removed some piece of apparatus which they particularly wanted to get hold of. Lloyd Owen felt he could well do it. As a kind of last fling, the L.R.D.G. would then re-enter the perimeter at dawn and destroy as many aircraft as possible on the two airfields there. This would be an important contribution to the plan, because dive-bombers were known to be based at El Gobi airfield, and dive-bombers could seriously upset the task of keeping Axis reinforcements out of the town, once it was taken.

Another task allotted the L.R.D.G. was the release of four thousand British P.O.W.s from the Tobruk cages. This was rather a sensational turn to the plans, and one which riveted much attention from the commandos. The idea was to arm the released P.O.W.s with captured weapons——much of them British—and get those who could not be transported away by sea out into the desert into the Jebel area, where they would link up with a mysterious 'X' force and operate as a guerrilla army far in Rommel's rear. This was to be known as Operation Bunghole.

The more the commando heard of the plan, the better it sounded. There was a simplicity to it which was appealing; perhaps their enthusiasm made it all seem a little too simple.

Inevitably, with the firelight flickering and glowing as a desert night wind stole through the scattered palms of the oasis, the commando asked, 'Who is this Colonel Haselden?' —the man whose plan it was to which their lives were committed.

The L.R.D.G. knew. More, the L.R.D.G. were willing to tell the commando what they knew. They had known John Haselden for a long time, almost for as long as they had operated in the desert. And it was plain that from their captain down to the last driver and radio operator, the L.R.D.G. thought the world of Haselden.

There was something about Haselden, some rare quality natural and unknown to the man himself, which inspired affection . . . a curious word to use between soldiers and a high-ranking officer, and yet it was there. Lloyd Owen especially had a regard for Haselden not exceeded by that for any other man.

He was a mystery man of the desert, a useful beginning to men strongly partisan to their commander. He flitted in and out of the lives of the L.R.D.G., always under rather dramatic circumstances, a man without a background, so far as they were concerned. In fact, there was probably little mystery about Haselden's background at all, even by their own statements; probably what they knew merely seemed inadequate to support their glowing regard for a very brave man.

His family had invested its fortunes in Egyptian cotton mills; in time John Haselden took over, living a pleasant, comfortable life in his white house on the banks of the Nile at El Minya. A man born in Egypt, of a Greek mother and British father, according to some, living his life in that country and yet remaining as so many do, more British than the most stay-at-home Briton.

War. John Haselden immediately offered his services where they would be most effective in the cause of Britain. Very quickly he became a British agent operating behind the enemy lines in the Western Desert campaigns.

Haselden was ideally equipped for such a rôle. He spoke Arabic fluently, and was known to Arab tribes for hundreds of miles up the desert. He could pass as an Arab even among Arabs themselves, and because of old desert friendships could rely upon protection and hospitality even where it was dangerous for his hosts to extend it.

Haselden, with other British agents, for long had been our eyes behind the enemy lines. In his guise as an Arab, he would be ferried by the L.R.D.G. well behind the fighting front and there left on his own. Weeks later another L.R.D.G. patrol would sneak through to some obscure rendezvous in the dreary scrubland, there to await the return of Haselden from his mission and bring him back to the British lines: sometimes they failed to recognize the bearded Arab who came out of the desert to join them.

He seemed not to understand fear. It was as though it never occurred to him that things might go wrong, that in some way the enemy would detect him. Certainly he never built himself up as a mystery man, or even as a man of outstanding ability and courage. Yet he had both.

On his last trip—to the Jebel—he had lived in a cave for weeks, almost within sight of the enemy. He had organized the local Arabs into a most efficient Intelligence service, not waiting for them to bring him scraps of information but instead detailing them to secure for him the information he wanted. At all times he ran the risk of betrayal by Arabs who would secure a big reward for his death or capture, but such was the hatred of the Libyans for their former Italian taskmasters that never once was Haselden's safety threatened. Or perhaps it was Haselden's personality that permitted him to live openly and without danger with the Arabs.

Sometimes Haselden, in search of information which his Arabs could not get him, would boldly enter enemy-occupied towns and camps, depending on his disguise to see him through. In the Jebel, too, he had once driven a flock of sheep across an enemy airfield, so as to examine the aircraft at close quarters. YI Patrol had come in to pick him up and bring him back to the British lines after his sheep droving exploit.

But it was a member of the commando itself who remembered Haselden's most daring exploit. This was the big Irish Guards lieutenant, Tom Langton, adjutant to the commando. Langton had been concerned in a dramatic attempt to kill Rommel, on the eve of a big desert battle.

Two submarines had crept up the African coast to a point not far from Rommel's headquarters at Beda Littoria, in Northern Cyrenaica. In them was a force of commandos under the command of Major Geoffrey Keyes, son of the famous admiral.

At an appointed time the submarines surfaced, to see a light blinking at them from the dark coast ahead. Langton said it was the surprise of his life to see the light blinking there exactly as it had been planned. He had helped to get thirty commandos ashore, though he had not landed himself. Holding the guiding light, with casual unconcern for the fact that he was bang in the midst of the enemy, was Haselden. He had been brought into the Jebel by a patrol of L.R.D.G. and had been scouting around Rommel's H.Q. for a fortnight.

Haselden led the commandos to a hide-out from which,

three nights later, they moved in on Rommel's H.Q. with the intention of killing the Desert Fox. The plan failed. Strong resistance was encountered. Later it was learned that Rommel had unexpectedly flown to Rome to attend his birthday celebrations with his wife. Most of the commandos were killed or captured. Keyes died in the raid; posthumously he was awarded the Victoria Cross. Haselden escaped into the desert, to be picked up by the inevitable L.R.D.G. patrol, operating hundreds of miles behind the enemy front line.

These stories and others were told around the camp fire; there was something of hero-worship about the telling, and it was as if there was a subconscious desire on the part of the retailers to win more support for their modest, friendly leader. Haselden was that kind of man—a man who made friends who tried to make friends for him. Whatever the result, at least it made the commando feel they were under the leadership of an exceptional man, an officer worth following.

The camp fires flickered low. The men grew tired of talking, and went to their blankets under the tall, stately palms that stirred softly above them as they fell asleep. And they slept. They slept deeply, unworried, the sleep of soldiers living for the moment and content not to look too far into the future . . .

VI

THE little ships—the M.T.B.s which were to thrust a landing force through Haselden's bridgehead at Tobruk—were in Alexandria, rehearsing the part they were to play. There were eighteen motor torpedo boats gathered to convey Force C into battle—two flotillas of fine, fast, American-built small boats: the 10th Flotilla under Commander Robert Allan, R.N.V.R., and the 15th Flotilla under Commander Denis Jermain, R.N. The whole to be commanded by Commander J. F. Blackburn, R.N., of *Ladybird* fame, the man who had run supplies into Tobruk at the height of the siege the previous year.

Off the coast of Cyprus, at a place which approximated to the conditions expected north of Tobruk harbour, Force A was practising night landings.

In both places disturbing events were causing officers to speak their minds. In Alexandria the M.T.B. commanders were scandalized at the little effort towards maintaining Security. In the two 'Tribal' class destroyers, *Sikh* (Captain St. John A. Micklethwait, D.S.O. and bar) and *Zulu* (Commander Richard T. White, D.S.O. and bar) rehearsing with a Marine Commando first in Palestine and then in Cyprus, they were dismayed at the little time given to practise landings.

The M.T.B.s found themselves having to make dummy landings under the interested gaze of civilian members of the Royal Egyptian Yacht Club, Alexandria. It seemed wrong to the officers concerned to announce their plans for a coastal landing from M.T.B.s in so flagrant a manner before the packed terraces of the Yacht Club.

For they were under no illusions as to the strength of the enemy fifth column in Alex. They knew that watchful eyes reported everything happening around the British Naval Base at Alexandria, and to advertise a seaborne landing was to warn the enemy to concentrate his defences upon no more than about three or four North African ports, of which only Benghazi and Tobruk were at this moment really important.

'Security,' the M.T.B. commanders were swearing, in a phrase that was becoming familiar throughout Operation Agreement, 'is the worst ever.'

And protests were made to higher-ups. Perhaps disconcertingly it was discovered that in higher naval circles there was also considerable unhappiness about the whole affair, and strenuous opposition was being made to the plan. Yet is was going through. Someone somewhere was driving it along, insisting that it be carried through even against the advice of high-ranking naval officers.

Alamein was looming ahead. Even where the plans for the big break-through were not yet officially known, sight of the fantastic supplies that were coming up the canal, as well as reinforcements through Tewfik, were sufficient to tell all with the slightest military knowledge that a big push was imminent.

When that push came, the Navy wanted to be in strength so as to play their usual effective part. They viewed with dismay the prospect of losing ships and men in a raid which seemed desperately hazardous, to say the least of it.

And a substantial part of the British Mediterranean Fleet was being committed to Operation Agreement. Eighteen M.T.B.s and three Fairmiles were to be employed to take in Force C. Two of our largest destroyers would carry in the marines and attached troops of Force A, and they would have escort from an ack-ack cruiser, H.M.S. *Coventry*, and eight 'Hunt' class destroyers. A cruiser and five other destroyers would bombard Daba on the same night purely as a diversion to Operation Agreement. And a submarine would also take part.

In view of the nearness of Tobruk to many important Axis airfields, the plan, which called for an occupation of the port for twelve hours and would keep the Navy under bombardment for up to thirty-six hours because of the need to withdraw troops and wounded, seemed certain to produce heavy Navy losses. And the Navy in certain quarters had strong feelings about losing ships on the eve of an important battle. They talked bitterly about the Beautiful Young Men of Cairo, with their enthusiasms and grandiose schemes, and their plans in everyone's mouths in G.H.Q.

The planners, however, had their answers. Smash Tobruk and it was better than a division in the field against the enemy. Losses had to be risked in order to make gains.

Grudgingly the critics agreed with them, so far. Certainly, if Tobruk could virtually be destroyed behind the enemy lines, it would ease the way for the Alamein break-out and the eventual destruction of the enemy in Africa in a remarkable way. But it was the planning of the operation that appeared to them to be at fault.

Apart from Security—and everyone was cynical about the attempts to keep plans secret from the enemy—it seemed to many officers that the whole thing was being taken half-heartedly, especially in the matter of practice landing exercises.

Opponents of Operation Agreement were most unhappy about the part to be played by the destroyers, *Sikh* and *Zulu*, and their marine commando. The Navy had some experience of landing troops from destroyers, but not too much, and not enough time was being given to practising the manœuvre, they felt.

They also felt that both destroyers should have been left to explore the matter of troop landings more intensively. As it was, the destroyers were not taken off from normal duties but had to fit practice landings in between routine submarine and other patrols. It gave little time to learning the many things that could go wrong in the complicated operation involved in the landing of approximately four hundred men on an enemy coast on a moonless night.

The practice landing off the coast of Cyprus had been harrowing. It had been found that the destroyers could not carry sufficient boats to take in all the marines and attached personnel on one trip. So it was arranged that half the personnel would be taken ashore at Tobruk, and then the boats would return to the parent ship to load up with a second flight of landing troops.

Faces became grimmer when the plan became known. Some officers were known to have sworn long and unpleasantly when they heard of the scheme. Presumably, they said sarcastically, the enemy in Tobruk—even third-rate Italian troops and German technicians—would have something to say about landing troops over a long period of time. What was required in a landing operation of this kind, they argued vigorously, was speed. An enemy must be taken by surprise; a foothold must be obtained before the enemy awoke to the presence of invasion. The marine commando should be thrown in in one swift, sudden assault, not in two widely separated groups.

But the destroyers just could not carry more boats on their crowded, limited deck space. If four hundred men had to be thrown ashore—and the planners in G.H.Q. insisted on that number—then they had to go in in two waves.

Off Cyprus faces became even more pessimistic as the marine landing was rehearsed. It was not the fault of the marines themselves. They were magnificent men, volunteers all and picked, finely-trained soldiers. They cheerfully endured the crowded conditions for the trip across from Haifa, and co-operated magnificently all the dark night long in the attempts to get them ashore.

It took an awful long time. The rehearsal promised anxious moments when the actual landing operation occurred. No one was too happy at the way events were shaping.

The only consoling thought was that rehearsals were always like that. Somehow nothing ever went right in practice operations, and yet somehow things had a habit of going pretty smoothly at the right, planned moment.

Sikh and *Zulu* finished their Cyprus rehearsal and went back to normal duties. Now that they were committed to the operation, like the M.T.B. skippers and crews in Alexandria, no one lost much time in worrying. This was just another naval operation a week or so ahead, and the Navy would go into the affray as determined, as resolute, and with all its traditional vigour uninhibited by personal criticism of plan details.

From the moment they knew that Operation Agreement had to go through, everyone concerned went ahead as if there wasn't the slightest possibility of failure.

There were critics outside the Navy, too. Some of these critics were doubtful about our Intelligence. They had heard a story—how true it was they never knew, but it was believed even in some quarters of G.H.Q. itself—that Operation Agreement was having added encouragement because of a report from a curious quarter about the strength of the enemy in this, its most important supply port, Tobruk.

The whisper—buzz, griff or gen, as it was more commonly known—spoke of a South African coloured soldier who had been captured in the siege of Tobruk. He had been put to work as a mess orderly in a German camp, and had somehow escaped and succeeded in reaching the Allied lines down the desert. Intelligence had questioned him about the enemy position in Tobruk. What they learned from the South African coloured soldier caused the planners to proceed much more boldly with the planning of Operation Agreement.

Not that the Intelligence obtained through one coloured soldier started the operation: that had been developing for weeks. But, said the critics, it had caused the plan to be expanded in size and in the scope of operations.

And many had doubts about the value of the soldier's report. They felt that he might have encouraged folly by underestimating the enemy strength; they felt that Haselden and his commando might be heading into a death-trap because of it.

For the South African soldier said that Tobruk was garrisoned by comparatively few Italian troops—about two battalions only, and they only third-rate soldiers. All else amounted to about a thousand German technicians and ack-ack personnel. A most modest force to attack.

If the report was true.

VII

IN Kufra, though the men slept soundly, a few officers had their moments of uneasiness. Captain Bray was one. He did not like this expedition; in fact, he thought so little of its chances that he had brought with him only four of his S.I.G., when, in fact, he needed about twice that number. He had a suspicion that some of the plan might have been betrayed to the enemy by Brückner or the dead Esser. And he had little faith in consequence in the S.I.G.'s own particular plan to capture a certain German general who was expected to be in the old Y.M.C.A. building in Tobruk. Not that it was important. The general was to be merely a trophy, something to display in Cairo afterwards as proof of the audacity of the raid.

Captain Lloyd Owen had his problems, too. He was able to discuss them with John Haselden; for they were old friends, comrades of many expeditions, and able accordingly to speak their minds to each other.

That last night in Kufra, watching the dying fires across the quiet oasis, Lloyd Owen said abruptly: 'John, you know that Security's been the worst ever for this trip?'

Haselden merely said: 'There's nothing I can do about it. We're committed. I have to go ahead as if Security has been perfect.'

That was something Lloyd Owen understood. But he worried for his friend and brother officer. He told him of the first time he had heard of the proposed raid. That was in Cairo, days before he had been summoned to Ops Room, G.H.Q., to meet a smiling John Haselden, full of his plans to discomfit the enemy.

'They were talking openly about this raid in bars and private houses in Cairo and Alex months ago,' the L.R.D.G.

leader said. 'The first news I had of it was in a private house.' It was the private house of someone concerned with the raid, but Lloyd Owen tactfully withheld that information at this moment. 'It seems impossible that by now the enemy will not be in possession of every detail.'

'You think they might be waiting for us when we drive into Tobruk?' Haselden laughed. Then he said abruptly: 'I have other worries, David.'

He waved his hand to encompass the sleeping commando. 'This isn't my idea at all. I never planned anything like this. In the beginning my suggestion was a simple act of sabotage, but the thing's grown out of all proportion—now it's a combined operation and I'm in charge of an essential part of it.'

There was no protest in Haselden's voice because of what had happened, no bitterness or recrimination. It was just a plain statement of fact, with a hint of bewilderment because of the situation in which he now found himself.

Lloyd Owen understood. He knew Haselden thoroughly and could understand his companion's feelings. He also remembered the original plan that had been put up to G.H.Q. by the British agent, and he agreed that it had been changed out of all recognition. It just wasn't a Haselden plan any longer, but the Nile cotton-mill owner was saddled with it.

The fall of Tobruk had shocked the Allied world; it had been so unexpected, so sudden. For a while there had been confusion in every man's thoughts in the Middle East, and then, as if spurred on by the reverse, every irregular unit in the desert began to plan to hurt if not capture the vital, strategic port. One plan had been to put folbotists into the harbour, armed with limpet mines, from the inevitable submarine. Tom Langton, of course, had been detailed for that raid, too; perhaps fortunately for him, because there seemed no plan to recover the folbotists, the submarine employed was Greek and it broke down outside Alex and had to limp slowly back. Other plans had been to sneak saboteurs in from L.R.D.G. vehicles.

That had been Haselden's plan. He had gone to G.H.Q.

with a proposition. If he could go to Tobruk with a few S.S. or other trained saboteurs—certainly no more than a dozen—he was confident that he could at least destroy the enemy bulk oil-storage tanks there and get safely away with the help of the faithful L.R.D.G. That was all his plan had been, and the men who knew Haselden knew it was a good plan, and it was a safe bet that he could pull it off.

Unexpectedly the plan began to find favour in curious places in the M.E. Command. All at once the bewildered Haselden found the plan taken from his hands and ballooned to the size of a combined operation. Half a dozen or a dozen commandos didn't seem enough for the planners; they began to think in terms of a squadron of S.S., and then they tacked on gunners and signallers and threw in a landing party of Argylls and R.N.F. After which it became a major expedition.

A marine commando was suddenly introduced into the planning, and with it destroyers, from which the commando would be landed, and after that came a flotilla of destroyers with an ack-ack cruiser to give cover to the troop-carrying destroyers. A massive raid by bombers was slung in for good measure. And a diversionary raid on Daba.

Even that was only the beginning. Enthusiasts decided to extend the idea to Benghazi. This would not be a major operation like the attack on Tobruk, nevertheless it would be quite a considerable raid planned for the exact hour of assault on that port. An assault on Jalo fortress and an attack on the airfield of Barce were planned simultaneously, to assist in the general embarrassment of the enemy, and even Haselden had to admit that the whole plan had much merit.

But the Security! Haselden knew it was as Lloyd Owen said—too many people were in the know. Too many tongues were wagging in Egypt. So far as September 13, 1942, was concerned there wasn't such a thing as Security.

But now they were committed to it. They were half-way to their destination, and they had to go through with the plan, whether the enemy knew about it or not. After their one brief discussion, neither Lloyd Owen nor Haselden referred to the matter again. They were soldiers. They had their orders. So far as the men were concerned, no one would ever have the slightest suspicion that their leaders were not absolutely brimful of confidence and overwhelmingly certain of success in the forthcoming attack.

Another officer felt in his bones that the enemy knew they were coming. He was the Royal Artillery lieutenant who had volunteered for this trip because it had occurred to him it was time he got himself some sort of decoration. What John Poynton had seen in Cairo had made him cynical about security.

He had found, for instance, that Q would not issue stores and equipment until they knew what they were intended for. 'Acting like nabobs,' was Poynton's wrathful description at the time. It was wrong, but Q were having to be told too much. Too many people were getting in on the planning.

He was also not very impressed with the move out. They had assembled with their vehicles at Abbassieh Barracks on the morning of August 24. It was broad daylight—with Egyptians as usual wandering around the camp in droves. Clearly they were a commando expedition readying for an assault somewhere. The sight of a naval rating wandering round swinging a limpet mine, in Poynton's opinion, at once restricted their possible destination to one of two or three places up the enemy coast. A smart observer would be no slower in forming a similar conclusion, Poynton was sure.

Not that it kept him from sleeping soundly. He was a man who seemed untroubled with nerves, and was enjoying this trip immensely as a change from static life with a coast defence battery. Besides, he was determined to get his decoration.

VIII

ON September 6 the commando, led by the faithful L.R.D.G., moved out of Kufra. The Hodden Grey kilt of Major Campbell was with them. Refreshed by their six days' rest, the men were eager to get on with the journey, and spirits were high as the convoy pulled north through the oasis.

The start was romantic enough. For miles they travelled through the palm trees of Kufra, among bald-headed, rounded red sandhills that threw, so early in the morning, long shadows across their path. The flies began to leave them, and the morning was not too hot in the first hour or so.

And then they hit the searing hot desert beyond Kufra and the hell started all over again. At first they travelled along an old Italian-marked track, but this was little advantage to them as it was in no sense a roadway but merely rutted sand. In fact, all that distinguished the track from the surrounding desert were the stakes or four-gallon oil drums set at intervals of approximately one mile (except where erosion had removed the markers) to show the way.

The temperature was hovering around 120° F. The dust rose, their throats were parched the instant the scalding hot desert wind swirled round them, and their skin seemed to shrink under the dehydrating influence of the blast. It was hell, and they had about eight hundred more miles of it— but no one thought of turning back. The show was on —their show, and they were impatient only to get on with it. In spite of the hardships, optimism soared and there was something of a picnic atmosphere in the party.

They hit some of the hardest going of their trek in the first hours after leaving Kufra. They had to cross a strip of soft sand that connected two mighty sand seas, the

Rebiana and the Kalansho, each several hundred miles in extent.

The L.R.D.G. knew the best way across, fortunately, but even the best way proved gruelling going. Once it took them several hours to traverse a distance of a few hundred yards. They had to travel across waves of yielding sand, each ridged wave fifty or more feet high, and at times almost precipitous-sided. The straining Chevrolets would slither in a sliding mass of sand down a steep slope, accelerate furiously before touching the valley bottom, and then attempt to climb the opposite sand bank without halting. Sometimes the ascent was so abrupt that the bonnets of their trucks scooped deep into the soft hillside, shoving the sand before them until the weight halted the laden vehicles.

Then it was a case of sand channels out, the metal strips being dug under the wheels to provide a firm grip if only for a moment; sweating, straining men threw their weight against the blisteringly hot metal sides of their wagons and manhandled them on to better ground. It was grim going, but the men never complained. There was even a masochistic sort of satisfaction in fighting the hard going, suffering, yet always winning through.

Climbing the loose sand ridges was only part of the problem. The tops were knife-edged, so that a frenziedly accelerating truck, triumphantly roaring up the slope without halt, might find itself breasting a rise and suddenly jumping clean out into space over what was almost a precipice—a dangerous possibility, and the commando quickly devised tactics to meet the situation. Generally, this meant driving along on to the ridge and holding to the high ground until a way down was discovered. Later they learned that Major Jake Easonsmith's parallel expedition to Barce had encountered similar razor-backed ridges and had suffered in consequence. A jeep had swept up to the crest, crashed over into the space beyond, and rolled over its two occupants. One had cracked his skull and lost his front teeth; the other was paralysed from the waist downwards. But fortunately Haselden's commando escaped such a disaster.

Later that day the L.R.D.G. came surely and certainly out of the wastelands up to a certain spot in the desert. It was a motor tyre. Their navigation was as good as all that; they could find a motor tyre in the thousands of square miles of signless desert.

The tyre marked a well. It had been placed over the mouth to hold back the sifting, drifting sand, but in this respect it had been largely unsuccessful. Now it was choked with sand. Some of the men, including two of the biggest in the party, Tom Langton and Private Glynn, went through the tyre to see what could be done. After some hot work digging, moisture began to seep through the muck at the bottom, but it was too fouled with animal droppings to be used and none was drunk.

On one occasion months earlier, fouled though the water had been at this well, Lloyd Owen's patrol had been glad of it. This was the only occasion when Lloyd Owen had noticed the appearance of that dreaded condition, *le cafard*, among his men. They had had an extended patrol under particularly trying conditions. Their water had all gone and for hours they had been without—and men don't live for hours in the Sahara without water and not begin to crack. He had seen the wild staring eyes of his men as the desert madness caught up with them, and he had prayed that his navigation wouldn't be at fault.

It wasn't. Suddenly they found the tyre in the desert. Thirst-crazed men got inside to dig away the choking sands. The well began to fill slowly. It was filthy water, but it meant life to them, and on that occasion it had been drunk.

This time Lloyd Owen brought them to the well merely as a navigational check; for they had sufficient ration of water in the jerricans for the journey ahead.

Early in the afternoon they arrived at the most northerly British outpost in the interior desert. This was Zighen. The post was manned by a tiny garrison of shiny-faced, black Sudanese troops, patiently doing their duty under conditions which would have been intolerable to most white men.

But from Zighen the going was good.   Between two great shifting sand seas is the Serir of Kalansho, a flat, baked-mud expanse that runs for several hundred miles north of Zighen, and which provides a fine, fast roadway up to the fortress of Jalo.   The 'roadway' is anything up to a hundred miles or more wide, but the interesting and inexplicable feature about it is that no matter how much the wind blows across the sand seas that surround it, drifting sand never accumulates on its surface.   The way is always clear and firm.

Now the commando made full use of it, covering forty exhilarating miles in little more than an hour before camping for the night.

This was their first camp north of Kufra, and now the drill for leaguering for the night was different, designed to evade possible detection by an enemy not too far away. Lloyd Owen did not seriously feel that they would be observed, but a wise man took all precautions.

In the journey up to Kufra leaguering had been rather a formality.   Trucks were reversed into small defiles or among rocks or bushes, less with an idea of concealment than as a protection against winds which sometimes blew up coldly in the night.   Camouflage nets, in fact, were not used until their first camp beyond Kufra.

But now, within a couple of hundred miles of enemy-held Jalo, in country which might occasionally be surveyed by patrolling enemy aircraft, the nets came out, vehicles were in close leaguer with each other, and there were no cheerful camp fires of petrol boxes at nights.   And for the first time sentries kept watch, too.

By the second day, speeding swiftly and happily towards Jalo Oasis, they were back in the old routine of desert life. Breakfast hastily prepared and eaten at first light, the commando was rolling as soon as possible to take advantage of the early morning coolness.   For three hours they would drive, then there would be a halt for a drink of lime juice, necessary on their restricted diet.   At this and every halt now, Lloyd Owen's radio operator set up the aerial and contacted the L.R.D.G. base at Kufra.   And at every halt

Colonel Haselden would go round to every truck and speak to the men and see that everything was all right.

After the briefest of halts for a change of drivers as much as anything else, they would drive on until about one o'clock. Then, where practicable, Lloyd Owen would take them to some known cover, such as overhanging rocks or bushes which could provide some sort of shade, and there they would tuck away their vehicles into the shadows, draping them with camouflage nets, and briefly lie up during the heat of the day. As a siesta there was little comfort for the men, but it gave them a short respite from the sun's powerful rays and conserved their energy for the last leg of their day's journey.

Usually a meal was taken before their very brief siesta. This was, inevitably, bully beef stew and biscuits, though generally they had tinned fruit, too.

An hour later, the men would be rudely summoned from their drugged repose; they would roll up the camouflage nets, climb into the wagons, and grind off into the open desert again. Generally they drove on until about half an hour before dusk, when Lloyd Owen would take them to some place he had remembered which would give good cover for the night's camp. It meant a long day for the men, a hardship that could not have been borne by less fit soldiers. But they stuck it out with wonderful patience and endurance, and every day saw them wanting to go on with their journey.

The evening camp, close leaguered under protective cover, with cooking fires screened from the open desert, was notably distinguished from other meals. For those who wanted it, a ration of rum was served. This was a time-honoured L.R.D.G. custom which was quickly embraced by every other irregular outfit operating in the desert.

The L.R.D.G. navigator would also set up his theodolite after dark, fix their position by the stars and tie it in with the dead reckoning calculations of the day. Meanwhile, and sometimes late into the night, the radio operator would be in contact with Kufra, reporting progress and accepting messages for possible transmission in case they ran into other wandering L.R.D.G. patrols in the desert.

On the second day out from Kufra the commando covered the better part of two hundred miles, and then made a brief camp until sunset. Now there was a ticklish problem confronting Lloyd Owen. It was necessary for the commando to be guided past the Italian post at Jalo without being detected, and Jalo sat uncomfortably close to the impassable Great Sand Sea. Lloyd Owen knew he would have to lead the commando through the gap between Jalo and the Sand Sea, and in daytime they would be quite visible to the Italian look-outs in the Jalo outpost.

He had decided to make the run during darkness, with all the problems attendant upon such an undertaking. The Benghazi party, incidentally, had announced their intention of making the run during daytime, at noon when a heat-haze distorted vision over distance on the desert. Lloyd Owen had argued with Colonel Stirling against the idea, but the S.A.S. leader went his own way. His force, as it turned out, got through without being seen.

When it was dark, weary though the men were from the day's grilling, the convoy took to the trail again. Without lights it crawled across the cooling desert through a moonless blackness, trucks almost touching each other in order to ensure that they wouldn't get lost. For hours they moved, trying to avoid all noise which would carry far across the night-still desert, holding their breath when a gear changed noisily, or metal clanked somewhere on metal.

Occasionally the vehicles became bogged down, and then silently cursing men got their tired bodies off the trucks and started the old process of manhandling them on to easier ground.

And then, all at once, the line of vehicles halted. A whisper came down the line.

'Tanks ahead!'

Eyes stared into the blackness, hands gripped the weapons so carefully tended on the trail. They sat taut and silent, waiting while the L.R.D.G. nosed ahead—into clumps of thorn scrub across their path.

It was a scare, but nothing more than that. Nerves

relaxed, men laughed in the darkness. The L.R.D.G. went slowly on, miraculously finding their way across the desert even in darkness. The convoy fell in behind them. A few miles away an Italian garrison slept, blissfully unconscious of the fact that at last, after travelling over one thousand four hundred miles, an Allied force had turned the enemy's flank.

A few hours later, still crawling through the blackness across a desert that was malignantly providing unusual obstacles to progress, the commando sustained their first loss.

Pilot-Officer Aubrey Scott must have dropped off to sleep, sitting on the side of his truck. Suddenly he fell overboard, landing on his shoulders in the sand. Scotty's bellow of alarm could almost have been heard back at Jalo. The truck stopped and a shaken R.A.F. officer came running up out of the darkness.

As he was dragged inboard again his comrades pointed out the advantages of Army over R.A.F. life. 'If you'd fallen out of your plane, Scotty, you'd have got yourself a lot more hurt.'

On they went through the night, an agonizingly slow journey. Then, forty or fifty miles north of Jalo, they leaguered down for a rest. They had been almost twenty-four hours on the move and were whacked. They crawled into their blankets, shivering because the night had been cold, seeking sleep even before food and drink.

They were on the move again at dawn, refreshed by no more than four hours' rest. But it was imperative that they should be well clear of the Jalo air patrol radius, which operated early each morning and then just before dusk. They sped on, watching behind them, but no plane appeared, and in time they relaxed and sought what comfort they could find. They had survived a moment of peril to their plans. They had crossed into enemy territory without detection. That day was fairly easy, but all the same evening camp was most welcome.

Major Campbell was by now in a thoroughly bad way. At every halt Colonel Haselden would walk back from

Lloyd Owen's truck, in which he rode, *kafired* like the Arab-looking L.R.D.G., concerned about his second-in-command. Wracked with agony, Campbell kept his suffering to himself and wouldn't accept any favours because of his condition. But his strength was rapidly going.

The fourth day out from Kufra proved hard but largely uneventful. They were now rounding the Great Sand Sea, the barrier that had been between them and Tobruk ever since leaving Cairo: it was this great, treacherous, shifting mass of loose sand, over six hundred miles long and up to two hundred miles wide, which was making the three-hundred mile direct route to Tobruk a journey of probably well over eighteen hundred miles.

They drove along the desert track which served between Jalo Oasis and another post at Jaghbub. There were signs of frequent use by enemy vehicles, and a strict watch was maintained in case they ran into Italian or German (most likely Italian) transport. But there was never a sign of the enemy all that day.

Camp was made at night by the deserted airfield known to the S.A.S. and L.R.D.G. as L.G.125—just a cleared expanse of desert on which aircraft, operating on secret missions with the desert units, formerly landed when Allied fortunes were higher than in those early days of September, 1942.

On September 10 the L.R.D.G. took them into a selected site at a place known as Hatiet Etla. There was nothing at Hatiet Etla except lots of close crowding, truck-high thorn bushes in a depression extending over several acres; but in a land where monotony is the keynote of existence and every cairn and almost every tree warrants a name, this was sufficient to grace the place with a title and a mark on the L.R.D.G. maps.

Again it was rest for the commando. They had three days to pass before their final move in on Tobruk, now only a short day's drive away, ninety miles to the north. They were ahead of schedule, but Colonel Haselden had insisted upon a goodly margin of time in case of unexpected difficulties and hold-ups during the desert traverse. Now his men put the time to good purpose, resting and recovering their energy again, and cleaning their weapons preparatory to the battle that they knew was bound to come within a matter of days.

Their spirits soared again as the trail weariness left them. Hatiet Etla was no convalescent camp, but for healthy commandos it was as good a place as any for a while, and certainly far better than the desert they had just crossed. Especially it cheered them to think they were almost through with desert travel. One more day of not too hard going, then the foray into a startled Tobruk . . . and then they would all withdraw nicely to a destroyer and be taken back to Alexandria. The faith of the commando in the Royal Navy was sublime. The Navy would be there.

The vehicles were most carefully leaguered and camou-flaged in Hatiet Etla. Lloyd Owen went round and selected a site for every vehicle and saw it was pushed into the shelter of its own drab desert bushes. They were well dispersed this time, too, occupying an area of several acres to make detection from the air all the more difficult. But that done, because they were hidden from the outer desert by the intervening dunes and scrub, they were pretty free with their fires and life was easy.

Hatiet Etla was remarkable for at least one thing: Captain Gibson's Celebrated Cold Cure.

Scotty wandered up to the M.O. one day, saying that his nose was snuffy. The R.A.F. bod had decided to catch a cold in the middle of the Sahara Desert.

The big, black-moustached Canadian doctor brooded for a moment, then came out with the remedy. 'Get yourself a shovel, then go and dig a bloody big hole in the desert. That'll sweat it out of you.' And he went on comfortably sitting on the two kegs of rum that were his charges during the journey up.

Scotty gave an indignant sniff and then walked away. He was thoroughly enjoying himself on this picnic, and what was a bit of a cold, anyway? Gibson could go and dig his own bloody holes. . . .

IX

THE officers had their first real conference about Operation Agreement at Hatiet Etla. In fact they had a whole series of them. During those days they went carefully over their plans, minutely considering every aspect and detail. Nothing was too unimportant to have the attention of their colonel—or, where it concerned the S.I.G., that of the meticulous Captain Bray.

When that was done to the officers' satisfaction, something like a rehearsal of the drive-in was staged among the bushes. Until this moment many of the men had been in ignorance of the actual planned approach to the enemy-held supply port; now it was all carefully explained to them.

They would enter Tobruk as P.O.W.s in three trucks only. The reason for this was the current Geman practice in conveying P.O.W.s, as Haselden and the L.R.D.G. well knew, having all too often been within close distance of British prisoners far behind the enemy line.

The enemy had less transport and fuel at his command than the Desert Army, and usually forty P.O.W.s were crowded into the back of a 3-ton truck when out on working parties. As it was, Haselden's commando would be rather lightly accommodated at less than thirty per truck.

But the question was how to get nearly thirty men into each vehicle in such a manner that their weapons, demolition explosives, radio sets and equipment were hidden from the view of a check-post sentry's glance over the tailboard of their trucks. That was the reason for the intensive rehearsal, and it was left to the officer commanding each truck to work out his own salvation.

This was effected in all cases by stowing equipment underfoot and then sitting over their weapons, with blankets stretched across their knees. The blankets would not be out of place, Haselden calculated. At that time of year, it would be rather cold riding in open lorries at dusk. For this reason, too, each officer had a flask of rum to hand round to the men during the drive in as a means of combating the cold night air; for they were dressed in their thin tropical kit, which though ideal for the burning heat of the desert day, was of little use in keeping them warm once the sun had set.

It took them a long time to dispose of themselves and all their kit in the three trucks, because they had a surprising amount of equipment. But in the end each truck commander reported himself satisfied. Not only were all the weapons out of sight, but they felt confident that if the balloon went up every man could instantly get into action with his firearms.

It was a protracted affair, this rehearsal, extending over a period of hours, but the men bore it patiently, recognizing that the success of their expedition—perhaps even their own lives—depended upon their hoodwinking the enemy the following day.

One minor problem was the lack of 'Germans'. For the drive in to Tobruk, Bray said they would need three Germans per truck. One would drive, one would sit next to the driver, and the third would stand on the seat, head and shoulders protruding through the cab roof, a German rifle covering the 'P.O.W.s' in the rear of the truck.

So Bray said, 'I want three volunteers. And you know the consequences if you are caught in German uniforms!' He looked round. He had plenty of volunteers; there was a mood of recklessness on the party now which made them volunteer for anything.

Lieutenants Barlow, Harrison and Langton were temporarily accepted into the German army. They were each issued with German overcoats and caps, and given German rifles and equipment. Then they were positioned as guards watching through the cab roofs over the 'prisoners'. The Palestinians took their seats as drivers or escorts, with Captain

Bray as a German officer in the front vehicle, and Lanark in the rear, also disguised as a German lieutenant.

It was then decided that another British officer should travel in the cab of one of the trucks with his hand thickly bandaged as if he were wounded. But the bandage could be slipped off in a second, and the officer would be grasping a hand grenade for emergency use all the way in to Tobruk.

Time after time the commando was rehearsed in the part it had to play. Captain Bray kept saying, 'Remember, you have been captured in the fighting at Alamein. You must look browned off, dispirited, worn out and weary.'

And he and Haselden showed the men how to sit slumped in their vehicles, with the right air of listlessness and apathy expected of men deprived of their freedom. It was not hard to achieve the effect. The men were bearded, scruffy from over a week without washing, their clothes grubby and desert-stained.

When the officers were satisfied, there was an impromptu drive-past with Haselden and Lloyd Owen carefully inspecting the men and their Afrika Korps signed vehicles. In spite of the seriousness of everything, both officers were laughing; there was something comical about it all, humorous perhaps because of the grim earnestness of the actors in their deadly rôles.

Haselden signalled that he was satisfied. The vehicles were carefully tucked away again, the men descended, stiff from hours in the trucks, and went to cook their evening meal. Then the glad tidings were brought to them.

They had too much rum! Not all could be taken into Tobruk. Either it had to be left with some of the surplus vehicles here in Hatiet Etla, or. . . .　　　'

The men were united in their views on rum left in an unappreciative desert, and when they had eaten their last supper in Hatiet Etla they shared the surplus liquor between them. It wasn't enough to make any man intoxicated, but added to their normal ration it was sufficient to create a festive air.

So, three hundred direct miles behind the Axis front line

at Alamein, the commando's fires blazed brightly in the night air, and they had a party that was joyful and without heed to the battle so soon to come. The officers, scarcely distinguishable in their grime and beardedness from the men, sat round the fires and joined in the singing and inevitable horse-play always attendant upon such occasions.

After a while even the Palestinians with Bray and Lanark joined the festivities. They had been held back by the meticulous Bray for a final run through of their part when they were stopped, as they expected to be stopped, at the check post in the barbed-wire perimeter of Tobruk the following evening.

Bray would be carrying documents which were calculated to get them through the perimeter. In addition he had a letter apparently written by some commanding officer at Alamein to a hypothetical officer in Tobruk saying that these prisoners were special ones and for that reason they must be put into the Tobruk cages without delay. That was to explain why P.O.W.s were being transported at dusk or afterwards.

All the documents carried by Bray, Lanark and the Palestinians had been cleverly forged in Cairo. Each carried the normal German's pay and soldier books, containing their photographs with and without hats. But in addition 'private' papers were most convincing.

Each carried letters from home, some of them love letters. The stamps, franking and envelopes were all German and therefore authentic. The love-letters had been composed by one of the S.I.G. who considered himself something of an artist in this direction. They had been rewritten by A.T.S. in Cairo to give the feminine hand, and the A.T.S. had also posed in civilian clothing to be photographed with the Afrika Korps uniformed Palestinians. All the Palestinians had proved themselves artists in posing in loving mood with their 'sweethearts'. Cairo had dubbed a Berlin background to each photograph, so that they looked authentic snapshots.

Weizmann's girl-friend (for the purpose of the picture) was an attractive A.T.S. who looked satisfyingly Aryan blonde. Weizmann gave her the name of Lisbeth Kunz in his love-letters, because that was the name of the daughter of a well-known Nazi who had lived in his street in Berlin before the war. Even this was done for a purpose. In case of questioning, it was better to claim some living person as a sweetheart—someone with an address and known background—rather than a flimsy hypothetical creature who could be destroyed by questioning and enquiry.

Their identities had been the source of much thought on the part of the S.I.G. officers. Each Palestinian was given a German, non-Jewish name to which he always answered. They had to memorize all the details in the documents, and were invested with a family background which they grew to know as if it really existed. Where they were 'married' they could repeat instantly the names and ages of their children, where their families lived and what work their wives were doing to help the German war effort. Every day either Bray or Lanark took them through this part of the deception. It was tiring, time-taking, and yet the Palestinians never faltered, never protested because they had less freedom on the way up than the rest of the commando. They at least were wholeheartedly committed to the task of destroying the German enemy.

In time the party grew tired of wrestling and singing and telling stories that all had heard before but pretended were new to them now. One by one they drifted to their blankets, stretched on the soft desert sand. Stars twinkled down on them from a moonless sky. The fire that had cheered them flickered less brightly, and then finally, slowly died into its own dreary ashes.

The last supper was over.

X

DAY for Operation Agreement was September 12, 1942. It was the day of the last supper in Hatiet Etla for Haselden's commando, and the time for embarkation of Forces A and C in Haifa and Alexandria.

It was also a time of anxiety for G.H.Q., Cairo. Weather reports covering the Tobruk area were disturbing. On the 11th, the day before, reports had stated that the sea was very rough—too rough for a landing operation involving small boats. On the 12th the reports were no better.

Finally an aircraft was sent up the coast to make a run in off Tobruk to have a look at the sea. Back came the depressing signal—white horses everywhere.

Then, at six in the evening, a special meteorological report suggested a bettering of conditions. Wind was down to 10 m.p.h., and the sea was becoming calmer. Withdrawn before despatch was a signal to Lloyd Owen in Hatiet Etla ordering a postponement of attack by Force B, Haselden's party. Operation Agreement was still on.

In Haifa, Force A had embarked aboard the destroyers, *Sikh* and *Zulu*—360 marines and twenty-two officers under the command of Lieutentant-Colonel Unwin, R.M., with attached troops inevitable for such an operation. There was a sub-section of 296 Company, R.E., a detachment of R.A.M.C. and Signals; and thirty men and one officer from 261 H.A.A. Battery, R.A. No coast defence gunners were taken aboard. Lieutenant Poynton, with Haselden's commando, would have been disturbed at the news.

Another man trying to reconcile the impossible with firm orders from above was the heavy ack-ack lieutenant, Philip Myers. He had been training with his thirty volunteers on

69

German and Italian guns at Mustafa Barracks, Alexandria, and he had been told he would have to bring eight captured guns into action when they took Tobruk.

Eight guns—thirty gunners. Big guns. It was just impossible. To crown it all, at the last moment aerial reconnaissance brought back photographs showing a further four ack-ack guns near to the beach they were to capture.

'You will man all those guns, Lieutenant,' he was told.

'With thirty men? Twelve guns? It's impossible,' said the young gunnery officer incautiously.

'You have your orders,' was the stern reply, and Philip Myers took his thirty men aboard the *Sikh* wondering what good orders were on a foray such as this when manifestly they were beyond possible fulfilment.

There had been changes aboard *Sikh* and *Zulu* since the landing rehearsal off Cyprus. Lieutenant Nickolls, R.N.V.R., returning to the *Sikh* after a spell in hospital, was not impressed by what he saw.

The two whalers had been moved from the davits abaft the break of the fo'c'sle, to auxiliary davits further forward. They had been replaced by motor lighters, while in the waist were six dumb lighters, stacked into each other rather like empty boot boxes. They were flat-bottomed, blunt-ended things made of plywood, abortions in the sight of any seamen. They had been made locally, in Haifa, by men who could have known little about boat-building and certainly had no pride in craftsmanship; for everything was crude, unfinished, with nails protruding everywhere, and cracks already showing behind splintered wood.

The two power boats, or motorized coffins, also specially built for the invasion were no more inspiring than the dumb lighters. At the moment there was a flap on, Nickolls learned—the engines had arrived late and were having to be fitted at the last minute.

The lieutenant had been a yacht broker in peace time, and he gave his opinion of what he saw. 'They may be all right for a dead calm on the Serpentine,' he said, and even that admission was grudgingly made. 'But if there is the slightest sea running they'll be hopeless.'

Yet an invasion was to depend upon them. Hundreds of men's lives were to be committed to those boats. It was beyond the understanding of the crews of *Sikh* and *Zulu*. The men simply called them 'bloody boot-boxes', or worse. To them it seemed as though someone had said, 'Make the cheapest boats possible. They won't be needed again.' That attitude of mind was baffling.

To the marine officers, though, what was much more perturbing was the thought that they would be using boats for this landing different from those they had practised on. At least, they thought, there should have been a rehearsal to include their untried and most uninspiring landing craft.

Even so, in spite of momentary misgivings, morale was high that Saturday night in Haifa harbour. The marines came aboard after dark; they were a cheerful bunch who impressed the crews with their vigour and spirit. They made themselves as comfortable as possible in very crowded conditions, and then the two destroyers slipped quietly away and made for Alexandria, arriving while it was still dark in the early hours of Sunday morning.

Security, everyone felt, had been perfect at Haifa. Captain Micklethwait, of *Sikh*, Senior Naval Officer, was sure there had been no leakage there in spite of months of planning on this and on an earlier invasion scheme.

For the Navy it had all started with a proposed landing at Sollum. Everyone thanked God when that scheme fell through, because it had seemed a remarkably hare-brained plan. Then had followed two months while the Tobruk raid was planned and rehearsed. Not very satisfactory months, for the Navy would have preferred to have spent all the time on landing rehearsals somewhere, say, down the Red Sea, but at least they felt that Security was first-class.

It might have applied to the Navy in Haifa, but Captain Micklethwait knew it did not extend to Alexandria and Cairo. Particularly Captain Micklethwait remembered, weeks before, an incident in the Gezira Club. Another officer, not in the least connected with the raid, wandered over to the destroyer captain, drink in hand, and said quite clearly, 'I say, old boy, I hear you're going to Tobruk.' And elsewhere, later, another officer told Captain Micklethwait the date of the impending Alamein battle.

Captain Micklethwait, a man who could not suffer fools, swore, 'What a bloody silly thing to tell a man who might be going in the bag!' For prisoners sometimes talked. Security *was* bad.

Coming in to Alexandria in the early hours of Sunday, September 13, there was another disturbing incident. As they tied up to a buoy, ammunition and oiling lighters came alongside, manned by the usual Egyptian port labourers.

One barefooted, spindleshanked son of the Nile looked up from a lighter and gave a cheerful hail to a *Sikh* rating: 'Hey, George, you go to Tobruk tonight, yes?'

The ratings talked about this among themselves. They felt annoyed. No one had told them anything, yet here the Arabs knew all about the show. In protest a petty-officer came with their grievance to the paymaster-lieutenant, Norman Elliott, who listened to them and then went off to report the incident to his commanding officer.

Sikh and *Zulu* sailed from Alexandria at 0545 hours that same day in company with four 'Hunt' class destroyers, *Hurworth*, *Beaufort*, *Exmoor* and *Aldenham*, while it was still dark. The Navy was not to be influenced by lightermen's inspirations.

On D Day, Saturday, September 12, Captain Norman MacFie, Argyll and Sutherland Highlanders, officer commanding Force C, had a minor problem posed him before embarkation. Two Greek officers had been attached to his company during the training period. The idea was to confuse enemy Intelligence, who might thus be led to think the rehearsals were for a contemplated landing on Crete or some Greek islands in the Mediterranean.

The Greeks had been enthusiastic about the deception. It was a job after their own heart. They had even shown up for a few minutes most—but not all—days, before retiring to the bars and admiring ladies of Alexandria.

Their enthusiasm was all the more because there was no need to carry deception to too great a length and they would not be required to get their fat, out-of-condition bodies ashore at Tobruk. Their rôle finished this day of embarkation. They came in to see Captain MacFie and pointed it out to him.

And then they asked the Scot for a letter to take back with them to show their commanding officer. They would even dictate the form the letter might take, they said helpfully. For instance, how pleased Captain MacFie had been with their co-operation. How well they had worked, and what prodigies of zeal and enthusiasm they had displayed for the arduous commando training of the past weeks.

They were encouraged because Captain MacFie smiled at them while they spoke. It was a pleasant smile. And afterwards he spoke pleasantly, too.

Captain MacFie was quite willing to write a letter for them. But, he said, he would be obliged to tell the truth. He would have to report that he had a low opinion of them, and that in his view they were a useless pair who should never be taking officer's pay in any uniform.

It was puzzling to the Greeks to hear MacFie, because the Argyll was smiling most charmingly and without offence while he spoke. But MacFie could smile and could sound pleasant, even when he was being untactfully frank.

In time the Greeks understood what was being said to them. There was momentary doubt, then a quick, shifting adjustment towards compromise.

'You will only give us a bad letter? Ha, but if we do not ask you for a letter you will not write anything bad about us? Yes? No one will know? Yes?' They beamed. 'Then we will not ask you for a letter, no?' It was settled. They shook MacFie warmly by the hand. They were men understanding each other. Then happily they trooped off to the nearest bar.   War sometimes took rather unpleasant turns, but they felt they had handled that crisis nicely.

MacFie had ninety-seven men and five officers in his company of Argylls.   Apart from a platoon of Royal Northumberland Fusiliers, Force C would also include two sub-sections of 295 Field Company, R.E., a detachment of A.A. gunners, under Lieutenant Beddington, R.A., and a captain and two sergeants of the R.A.M.C.

MacFie had enjoyed the training for the Tobruk raid. It had all started on Ruweisat Ridge, early in August. The Argylls were in the line at Alamein, digging in to face Rommel's next expected assault.   Colonel McAlister, commanding 1st Battalion Argyll and Sutherland Highlanders, had sent for the ' D ' Company commander and said, 'I have to send a company off on some secret operation. I don't know anything about it.   How do you feel about taking it on'?

MacFie, restless because of a period of static warfare, jumped at the opportunity.   'I'll go with pleasure, sir,' he said.

Next day he and his company moved off to Amiriya, near Alexandria.   Three days later a signal took them to Cairo.   The following day the company was sent back to Alexandria.   The operation was going nicely to plan, everyone felt.

But then had followed most interesting training.   Every day a number of men went aboard some M.T.B.s and were taken on a normal submarine patrol into the Mediterranean. The idea was to get the men used to sea and free from the effects of seasickness.   At night they went out on M.L. patrols. As a variation, they sometimes put out to sea in clumsy, rolling caiques, and stayed just outside Alexandria harbour all night, at first in awful misery because, in the opinion of the Argylls, Caiques Were Cows.

Landings were also made, sometimes in the seclusion of a cove around Alexandria harbour, sometimes for the benefit of Yacht Club members.

Interesting, if somewhat arduous, was the training inside

Mustafa Barracks itself. There was weapon drill, unarmed combat, and constant rehearsal in the task before them.

Part of the task appeared to be the capture of enemy guns—big guns. Time after time they rehearsed the operation, sometimes after dark. A five-foot high ring of sandbags was the gun position inside Mustafa Barracks. Argylls crept up to this from all angles, positioned a tommy-gunner outside the one narrow entrance, and then grenades were tossed inside. The Argylls were betting that grenades tossed suddenly into a gun pit would send enemy gunners stampeding out through the one narrow exit; their calculations further assumed that few gunners would survive if the one opening was covered.

But at this stage they were not told where they were going or what the task was before them.

On D Day the Argylls came down to the dock area in trucks to which were fastened, for all the world and a fifth column to see, the collapsible boats to be used in their landing. Morale was high, as was to be expected from the Argylls, and the men were looking forward eagerly to their job. They were wearing K.D. shorts and shirts, commando rubber-soled boots, and carried a small pack and water bottle each. For weapons they had a choice selection which ran from rifles to Bren guns, and covered commando knives and grenades.

There were nine sections, one to a boat, with Captain MacFie's H.Q. section in another M.T.B. The commanders of the vessels looked cheerfully young, but inspiring for all that in the way the Navy always inspires landlubbers.

When they were aboard they were told where they were going. After which they got down to 'kip' or play cards.

There was another officer with a last-minute problem to disturb him. He was Ernest Raymond, the lieutenant commanding the platoon of Royal Northumberland Fusiliers. He was not saying complimentary things about Higher Authority at all.

He had a feeling they were going on a suicide trip, yet

someone had made a most unfortunate last minute change of plans, affecting the prospects of his platoon of machine-gunners.

Right at the very last minute one M.T.B. had been withdrawn from Force C, and Raymond's machine-gun section had clicked for this—it was their M.T.B. that had been taken from them. This was no way to plan a landing, Raymond exploded, when told.

At three in the afternoon he had got his thirty-two Geordie lads aboard some 3-tonners at Mustafa Barracks, along with their heavy loads of ammunition, guns and equipment, and been driven down to the docks. There he had had his first intimation of the change in plans.

All these weeks they had rehearsed landing from six M.T.B.s. Now they were told that only five were available to the R.N.F.—seventeen only would comprise Force C and not eighteen as had originally been planned.

Raymond was profane, and his men listened in silent admiration. But it was most disturbing. The plan called for the landing of troops from the M.T.B.s in rubber dinghies, awkward things to manœuvre even in the most placid of circumstances. And the R.N.F. had a fantastic load to get ashore, apart from themselves. They were carrying 100,000 rounds of ammunition for their four hungry Vickers guns—each man's share was 84lbs, apart from their weapons. Raymond worried about the problem, wondering how to redispose his forces so as to get them all safely ashore.

Promptly at 17.50 hours, Force C left Alexandria harbour. It was, fortunately, daylight, or the members of the Royal Egyptian Yacht Club might have missed this brave sight, which would have held an element of unfairness considering their wholehearted support of the previous weeks' dummy landing operations.

XI

IT was six o'clock . . . reveille . . . with the sun already up and warming the dreary scrub surroundings that justified an importance on a map. Hatiet Etla on the morning of September 13, the day of the attack.

It was a day no different from any other in the past weeks. There was the sun streaming down on them from a cloudless sky. There was a dancing of the horizon where hot air currents even so early distorted vision. There was silence, vast and completely unbroken until the stirring of the men about the camp.

Then they began to tramp in from places where they had slept, dirty, dusty blankets slung over their shoulders, and mess tins ready for breakfast.

It was a day no different from any other, and yet the men knew it was different, and already a tension was beginning to take hold of some of them. Even the ones who seemed unconcerned often betrayed an inward build-up of nerves by being too elaborately, too obviously unconcerned. Few men were quite as usual, that bright September morning.

Breakfast was quickly taken. As much to eat as they wanted now, with rather more to drink than on other mornings . . . *chai*, over-sweet, brackish with a too-generous tea allowance—wonderful *chai* that put the heart into a desert warrior and made him a new man again.

A briskness began to sweep over the camp. The first, pre-breakfast listlessness—perhaps a faint reaction to the previous night's party—was wafted away. There was noise and cheerful camp sounds as the men piled kit on to the trucks and mounted ready for the drive out. Lloyd Owen's L.R.D.G., efficient desert campers, were already in their Chevs and waiting, the wind of the morning stirring the folds of their colourful Arab head-dresses around swarthy, bearded, Arab-like faces.

Haselden was moving about the camp, talking, smiling, quietly joking, received with pleasure wherever he went. Captain Gibson was with Major Campbell. The London Scot was so weak it was painful to watch him. But he was shaking his head again, resisting the advice of the Canadian doctor. No power on earth was going to take Colin Campbell out of this fight.

Three trucks were going to be left in Hatiet Etla. They would move out in four Chevs, dropping one later in the day as they approached the Tobruk perimeter. That was just in case of accidents; just in case one of their trucks at the last minute developed a fault . . . they would have a spare to get them through.

It was planned that at some later date an L.R.D.G. patrol would cross the desert to retrieve the trucks, but for the moment they were immobilized so that if the enemy discovered them first they would be useless to them. Lloyd Owen removed the distributor heads; then, with the whole commando watching because they knew their lives might depend upon it, he buried each distributor head by the front offside wheel of its respective truck. If things went wrong with the commando and some had to break out into the desert, at least they would know how to get the 3-tonners into action again—if they managed to reach Hatiet Etla.

All the spare kit was left in the three camouflaged vehicles, together with food and water and reserves of petrol calculated to get them back to Kufra. Then, with a last look round at the camp that had been their home for three pleasant days, Colonel Haselden climbed into the leading L.R.D.G. truck alongside Lloyd Owen, and the patrol leader began to take them out into the desert again.

Six L.R.D.G. vehicles slowly bumped their way up on to more open ground; four 3-tonners ground their way up the sandy slope in their rear. The men settled back, overcrowded and not too comfortable. The last lap had begun. One more halt, they had been informed, and then they would part with the L.R.D.G. and take the plunge of entering the Tobruk perimeter. The commando was unusually quiet that morning.

Hatiet Etla was about ninety miles south of Tobruk. The going was good over the open, scrub-covered waste-land, and they kept easily to schedule. They travelled very slowly so as not to raise any cloud of dust which might fail to disperse in time if any enemy aircraft was sighted, and they moved in very open formation.

The L.R.D.G. kept a course well ahead of them, almost out of sight at times, while the four bigger Chevs moved in a big square, each vehicle separated by about three hundred yards from any companion.

Neither the L.R.D.G. nor the commando was much concerned about being detected, however, for they had moved into the old battlefield south of Tobruk. Here, in every direction as far as they could see, were thousands of shot-up guns, tanks and vehicles, many of them identical with their own. If a plane came over, all they need do was halt until it was out of sight. A few more Chevs would attract little comment in such a confusion.

By about eleven-thirty they saw that the L.R.D.G. had halted and were waiting for them by some piled-up rocks. When they got near, the lighter vehicles led the way into some cover that was merely a depression in the earth's sur-surface. They debussed. Fires were started and a meal and brew-up were prepared. Then they got down to 'kip' for the next four or five hours.

They were only about thirty-five miles from Tobruk now.

Time dragged. There was too much in their thoughts for the hot afternoon to seem tolerable as a siesta. Most of the men dozed, though a few fortunate extroverts slept— and slept noisily.

Approaching four in the afternoon, someone couldn't stand it any longer, but rose and started to make a fire. Tea went on. The movement brought other men sitting up. Then they, too, rose from the hot sand and trudged heavily to make their own fires. By four o'clock the camp was alive again, and feeling better for moving about. A meal was made and eaten; tea was swilled down. Then once more the air of tension began to mount.

Still they kept to their four trucks—even now one could fail them and jeopardize the whole expedition. With only the briefest word of command from their officers, they climbed the hot metal sides of their Chevs and settled down again. The L.R.D.G. pulled out. This time Haselden was riding in the leading 3-tonner, no longer with the L.R.D.G. The parting of the ways had already begun.

Once more the desert, bumping, lurching across it, uncomfortable but thinking nothing of it. If they had thoughts at all it was of a few hours ahead, when sunset came and they went into Tobruk. They looked at the sun often now. It was still very hot, still high in the sky, but it was descending. They had only a few hours of light left.

They travelled with still greater caution now, driving more slowly, with every man watching for first sign of the enemy. Then they saw it.

A plane was skimming low over the horizon ahead of them. It disappeared from sight. Men relaxed. Right ahead must be an enemy airfield, probably the one at El Adem, close to Tobruk. Later they saw another plane come in to land, and now it was nearer and seemed much bigger.

Lloyd Owen's L.R.D.G. were far ahead on the horizon again—so that if they ran into an enemy patrol it need not necessarily prejudice the commando's prospects. After a while someone in the leading 3-tonner said, 'The L.R.D.G. have stopped.' They knew what that meant.

The four trucks closed in on the six stationary desert patrol vehicles. The commando could see that every *kafired* head was turned, watching them as they came up. There was something about the bearded faces—something some-how faintly uneasy, concerned and not a little depressed —as the 3-tonners slowly halted near to the L.R.D.G. The commando guessed how their trail companions were feeling, now that the parting had come.

Bill Barlow, the ack-ack gunner officer, swung out of the rearmost 3-tonner and called, 'Everyone off. Into your positions on the other trucks.'

A wind was beginning to blow, cold and cheerless though the sun still had warmth. The men found they were already feeling cramped and cold, and they vaulted out of the truck, glad of the excuse for movement. Arms and ammunition were handed down to them, and they began to take their places on the remaining three trucks. The driver of Barlow's truck drove it against some bushes, which partly hid it. Then he put the distributor head under the sand by the front offside wheel and came back to join the others.

Barlow's truck was a write-off. The L.R.D.G. weren't going to bother to try to recover it, so near to the enemy base. In any event, in the last few miles it had shed its fan belt—the only mechanical mishap to any of the Chevs in their long desert trek. Still, the truck was good for an emergency last gallop, and everyone made a careful note of its situation in case they had need of it later.

On the trucks, the men realized why Lloyd Owen had stopped. They were within sight of the Axis road.

Three or four miles ahead of them they could see tiny, crawling dust-clouds on the northern horizon. It was the perimeter road; the transport would be the enemy.

Lloyd Owen came walking back from his truck. Haselden and Campbell went slowly forward to meet him. Then Langton and Bray came up to say their good-byes. For a few moments the party stood together, shivering in the growing night wind, and discussing radio contact arrangements in a rather desultory manner. They all knew they were putting off the moment of actual parting, but it had to come.

Haselden said, 'Well, good-bye, David. Thanks for everything.' He was smiling, his eyes twinkling. There was no fear, no lack of confidence in John Haselden, at that moment.

They shook hands all round, a very ordinary parting,

after all. Then everyone went back to their vehicles. There was a roar as a starting engine shattered the quiet of the desert. The other two trucks added to the noise. A gear was engaged, a Chev lurched forward. Truly this time they had entered on the last lap.

As the three 3-tonners crawled past the line of L.R.D.G. vehicles there was a momentary silence. Every *kafired* head watched broodingly, unhappily, as their trail companions surged by. The L.R.D.G. knew what lay ahead for the commando. They knew that some who sat there on the crowded trucks would never see another day. And they felt suddenly regretful, as men do at such times, wishing they had been more tolerant, less impatient, especially in the beginning of the desert trek when the commando had suffered so much with their more awkward vehicles.

Lloyd Owen watched the silent commandos and thought, 'I wish we'd been kinder to them. They're fine, brave men.' He felt unutterably depressed.

Then some commando broke the spell—a spell which had only lasted seconds, anyway. He called a parting farewell to an L.R.D.G. crony. Someone else shouted something that was well-meant if crude. At that the whole commando woke up. Everyone shouted good-bye. Someone started a cheer for the L.R.D.G. All at once the sentiment of parting was brushed away by men who were very little sentimental, anyway.

The three 3-tonners trundled into the scrub desert, their occupants noisily cheerful, if too crowded for comfort. They seemed brimful of confidence, completely sure that they were embarked upon a mission of success. The last thing the L.R.D.G. heard as the trucks pulled away was . . . laughter.

There was no laughing, no cheering, not even shouts of good-bye from the L.R.D.G. They knew what faced the commando: they had their own work to do that night, but it was just within the perimeter; *they* didn't have to place themselves right in the heart of the enemy defences, as was the commando plan.

Their bearded faces followed the 3-tonners, watching them until they were specks on the darkening horizon. They sat and shivered in the stiffening breeze, without even the will to stir themselves and drive into a more sheltered position.

In time, though, Lloyd Owen did make a move. He turned in his seat. He was planning the next hours ahead. They would find a hide-up until it was time for them, too, to break through the perimeter. . . .

Lloyd Owen suddenly snapped out of his depression. His startled followers heard a warning shout from their captain; they swung round instantly and followed the direction of his pointing finger.

Shocked, they saw a dust cloud on the desert, moving parallel with the receding commando. A dust cloud . . . it could only be the enemy. And though it was moving parallel with the commando vehicles, the L.R.D.G. saw instantly a danger, the possibility of an interception, perhaps along the escarpment.

Six 30-cwt. trucks roared into life. Wheels spun and threw up miniature storms of sand and dust as gears were slammed home. The L.R.D.G. forgot their vague, momentary mood of 'browned-offness' and went into action.

They tore in at the enemy—an Italian patrol of several cars, they saw as they closed. The swelling roar of their engines attracted attention. For some reason the Italians stopped and some even got down to look back at the approaching L.R.D.G. patrol.

Then the L.R.D.G. saw movement, saw the Italians begin to run frantically back to their vehicles. Their identity had been guessed.

The L.R.D.G. came rocketing in, guns opening up as soon as they were within range, the wild-looking, bearded, Arab-head-dressed L.R.D.G. shouting in the excitement of the moment. The Italian cars began to move. Bullets got them. They stopped. Italians began to fall out, screaming. Some got to their guns but the fast-moving Chevs circled the patrol and silenced the opposition.

Within seconds the battle was over. The swiftness of their attack had won the day for an L.R.D.G. which didn't suffer a scratch.

They questioned an Italian prisoner. What was the strength of the Tobruk garrison?

The terrified Italian told them that his patrol was part of a division which had been moved into the Tobruk area within the past twenty-four hours. He also thought that strong German reinforcements had been unexpectedly pulled back to Tobruk recently, too.

XII

AFTER over twenty-four hours at sea, Lieutenant Ernest Raymond, R.N.F., was feeling fine. All through the night of Saturday into Sunday sixteen M.T.B.s and three Fairmiles had sailed as if heading for Crete, travelling at comparatively slow speed. Only sixteen M.T.B.s now. Outside Alexandria the seventeenth had broken down and the personnel had been transferred to an M.L. They were R.N.F.—Raymond had clicked again. But by now he wasn't bothering.

When day dawned they had found themselves in a fairly tranquil sea, with the sun shining delightfully, so that most men came up to enjoy a sunbathe. There was no sign of the enemy all that peaceful day.

Now evening was closing in on them, and as soon as it was dark the two long columns of vessels would change course and head in for Tobruk at tearing speed.

But for the moment, peace. True, Raymond thought little of their prospects of survival. He had written a letter shortly before embarking, 'Dear Dot, I don't think I shall be returning from this trip. . . .' It was to be posted if he failed to return.

Raymond's opinion was that the R.N.F. and Argylls were expendable. The plan seemed reasonable enough if Haselden's commando captured a bridgehead, then he was pretty sure Forces B and C combined could smash their way along the south shore of Tobruk harbour as far as the bulk oil-storage tanks.

That was all right. He was also confident that the R.N.F. would do their particular job successfully, too. Their task was to get to the Acroma Crossroads, mount their four Vickers machine-guns, and hold off all enemy reinforcements from the desert. Lying on his back in the late afternoon sunshine, Raymond was not bothered about that part of the programme, either.

He was a man fanatically proud of his regiment, a man who thought his Geordie boys the salt of the earth and the pick of any troops anywhere. He could even feel patronizing towards MacFie because his men talked a different tongue from the Tyneside dialect. Though Scots were pretty good fighters, he would admit tolerantly.

And confident in his men, sure there was no weak link anywhere in his platoon, Raymond simply did not worry about their ability to hold off the enemy for the twelve hours required. Good Lord, he would tell people, the R.N.F. had been in every desert battle right from the start. As the only machine-gun regiment in the Middle East, weren't they always thrown into the thick of battle?

Of Raymond's company, which had seen action from the commencement of Wavell's first push and throughout the Siege of Tobruk, it can be said that it had a fighting record second to none. Its decorations numbered thirty-six and ranged from a V.C. downwards. In the platoon both section commanders had the Military Medal, and there were four other Military Medals, including Raymond's batman, Fusilier Preston. Later Fusilier Chambers was to get the D.C.M., M.M. and bar.

They had spirit, the northern boys. The best in the world, Raymond would say. When he called for volunteers for a secret mision, the whole platoon had stepped forward. When he had said that only swimmers would be taken, all the non-swimmers had immediately taken lessons.

Raymond remembered Fusilier Pratt, who had nearly drowned in swimming training. Fished out, gasping, he had refused to come off the expedition. And Raymond's platoon sergeant, Bell—he should have been left behind, but had refused point-blank to do so.

The spirit was all right, Raymond thought comfortably. For an action like this he had a well tried team, the best little bunch anywhere. As for holding Acroma Crossroads,

Lieutenant-Colonel John Haselden, the leader of Force B,
photographed under the wing of a Lysander at Kufra

An historic L.R.D.G photograph of Haselden coming out of
the desert hundreds of miles behind enemy lines, after the
exploit which included driving sheep across an enemy airfield

L.R.D.G vehicles follow a rough track on their way to Kufra

A typical desert scene showing an L.R.D.G. patrol resting after
strenuous labours in soft sand

'Ahead, enemy vehicles sped by the watching commando'

A photograph taken during a halt for a meal on the long
journey from Kufra to Tobruk

Hatiet Etla. The last supper on the eve of the attack

Four M.T.B.s such as this were lost in Operation Agreement. All the other twelve in Force C were more or less severely damaged

An aerial view of Tobruk taken
some time after the raid

A remarkable night photograph
taken during the raid as R.A.F.
Wellingtons score direct hits on
two of Tobruk's jetties

The target for the Marine commando – the piers on the north shore
of Tobruk harbour

The wrecked *San Giorgio* which, as a fort ship, helped drive off the
M.T.B.s. The boom defences can be seen top right

Zulu comes in under heavy fire to tow off *Sikh*

An artist's impression of a gallant Naval action

This picture of *Coventry* was taken only a matter of hours before
the attack which crippled her

Eleven-forty, September 14, 1942. *Coventry* on fire and sinking,
with some of her crew already in the water, abandoning ship

Survivors from *Coventry* being helped up scrambling nets on a destroyer

An enemy photograph of survivors from *Sikh* being brought into Tobruk harbor on an Italian barge

Major Colin Campbell

Captain Norman MacFie

S.S.M. Arthur Swinburn

Lieutenant George Harrison

Captain David Lloyd Owen

Captain John Gibson

Captain Peter Powell

Pilot-Officer Aubrey Scott

Lieutenant Ernest Raymond.
A photograph taken on the
return journey from Tobruk

Lieutenant Bill Barlow

Lieutenant Michael Duffy

Lieutenant John Poynton

they'd do it, he thought. No one would get past the R.N.F. that night. The only shadow of doubt in his mind came when he remembered the plan to pull them out when the action was over.

He knew it was impossible. An M.T.B. was supposed to be coming in to take them off, but though Raymond had told all this to his men he didn't believe in it himself.

No retreat would be possible, he was certain. At the best they would go into the bag, as a result of this operation. At the worst, dear Dot would get her letter.

He went down below. Captain Cuseter, the doc, was seasick. It tickled the Geordies. The M.O. was sick. They were even prescribing for him, and it was all M. & D. (medicine and duty).

Captain Cuseter's medical orderly had also been in the picture, earlier. This was when the youthful M.T.B. captain, Lieutenant Charles Coles, R.N.V.R., had instructed his passengers in the various drills in case of fire, air-raid or need for abandoning ship.

The R.N.F. had co-operated enthusiastically, but not so the R.A.M.C. sergeant. Lieutenant Coles was surprised to find he had shipped a non-combatant. The sergeant came forward and said so. He was very polite, but also very firm about it. He could take no part in such drills because, he announced, he was a non-combatant.

It was a highly interesting situation, but Coles took it tolerantly. Some time later the non-combatant was to provoke a further highly interesting situation.

So they sped on, hour after hour, with the sun dropping over the unseen land to the west of them. Nice enough to be a holiday, but they knew it wasn't going to be one. Still, Force C was ready for it.

Curiously, Lieutenant Raymond was in complete ignorance of the existence of Force A. Someone had forgotten to tell him they might run into a marine commando in the dark.

As darkness fell, Corporal (acting Sergeant) M'Guigan of the Argylls was feeling delighted with the trip. He had played cards almost incessantly since leaving Alexandria. It was three-card brag, and he couldn't go wrong. When word came below to pack up and prepare themselves for some high-speed travelling, he had won £12 10s.

For some time M'Guigan looked at his money and debated its future. He was going ashore with a good mob, but he had a feeling things were going to be tough for them that night, in spite of the smiling confidence of their commanding officer. After a while he decided to hide it on the M.T.B. It would be safer than on his person, he thought.

Corporal (acting Sergeant) M'Guigan made one of the biggest mistakes of his life there.

Commander Blackburn was in Commander Jermain's M.T.B. With the last light of D1 day, he looked round. Two columns of boats were keeping perfect formation. They were running easily on their auxiliary engines. Commander Blackburn scanned the darkening sky again and was satisfied. He was quite sure that at no time had they been observed by the enemy. He gave an order.

Both columns turned. They were heading towards Tobruk now. Force C was going into battle.

Force A had been detected by the enemy during the morning. *Sikh* and *Zulu*, with an escort of four 'Hunt' class destroyers, had rendezvoused with a Force D somewhere north of Aboukir Bay at about 0925 on D1, September 13.

Force D, whose function was a normal one of giving anti-aircraft cover to the force as a whole, had left Port Said the previous evening; it consisted of the ack-ack cruiser, *Coventry* (Captain R. J. R. Dendy, R.N.), and another four 'Hunt' class destroyers. The two forces met on opposite courses, turned north, and immediately took up cruising dispositions.

At 09·30 the *Coventry's* long-range radar picked up an unidentified aircraft flying about thirty to forty miles west of the combined force, on a north-westerly course and climbing. A squadron-leader from the R.A.F., attached to

Coventry for air liaison purposes, looked at the plot and gave his opinion that it was friendly, probably an aircraft of P.R.U. (Photographic Reconnaissance Unit) making a run up the enemy-held coast. Certainly the plane did not seem interested in them and was making no attempt to get nearer. For some time the plot was watched, then the signal faded.

All the same, Captain Dendy maintained a course to northward to confuse the aircraft if it were a hostile watching them. Then, at 1110 hours, he received a signal from Alexandria stating that it was suspected that the enemy had spotted Force A. At 1240 came another signal confirming the suspicion. An intercepted enemy radio communication made it clear that they had knowledge of the presence of both Force A and Force D.

Captain Dendy maintained the northerly course for some time, and again the enemy must have obtained knowledge of this, because at a much later date the *Coventry*'s captain learned that the garrison at Rhodes had been alerted that day. But if Force A were to reach their release point on time this false course could not long be maintained, and about 1015 Captain Dendy altered course and turned west.

It was a beautiful September day, a peaceful Sunday with no incidents, no aircraft alarms or enemy action of any sort as they travelled steadily parallel to but out of sight of the North African coast. *Coventry*, the biggest ship, was in the centre of the force, with *Sikh* and *Zulu* on either bow and the eight 'Hunts' protectively maintaining stations around them.

At nine o'clock that evening came a signal to all taking part in Operation Agreement. It was from the Prime Minister, Mr. Winston Churchill. It was simple and direct, wishing good luck and all success to those taking part in the attack. It was received and transmitted to personnel in Forces A and D, but neither Force C, in the M.T.B.s, nor Haselden's commando received it.

At this time, 2100 hours, *Sikh* and *Zulu* parted from Force D and went towards Tobruk. Captain Dendy at once reduced speed to sixteen knots, to let the two 'Tribal' destroyers get ahead, so as to confuse enemy radar about their progress. Then he turned Force D, now including the other four 'Hunts', eastwards, increased speed to maximum to clear the area, and headed for Alexandria, all in accordance with orders.

Shortly before 2130 hours, a bomber crossed overhead. After that there was a continuous stream of them, flying westward in a steady procession. They were showing identification signals. It was 205 Group, on its way to bomb Tobruk.

The kick-off would be any minute now.

Just outside Tobruk Harbour a submarine surfaced cautiously. After a few minutes it made signal to base, saying, 'Weather conditions suitable for landing.' Then it settled down again on the ocean bed to pass the next four hours until the time for assault by Force A.

XIII

THE commando was already behind time. The escarpment had proved difficult to negotiate, and the three trucks had crawled along its edge for half an hour before finding a reasonable way down to the lower level. The delay—a sudden, panicky feeling that now they were also in a race for time—built up the tension in them, a tension which steadily grew as the trucks bumped slowly, tediously over the rough ground towards the Tobruk road.

Not all appeared to be troubled by nerves, however. Duffy and Graham Taylor among the officers seemed unconcerned. Tom Langton, dressed in the German overcoat that would have him shot instantly if captured, pulled faces at his 'prisoners' and appeared to be enjoying the ride. And many of the men seemed indifferent to their surroundings, and concerned only to get a cigarette lit in the breeze. Others were already throwing out hints for the rum, but though they were cold in spite of the blankets over their knees, the time was not ready for the warming alcohol.

Suddenly everyone grew tense. As they trundled over the rough scrub towards the road, they saw two German light trucks scudding towards them. The two parties would nearly meet. Every head turned to watch, waiting for the Germans to slow down; hands grasped weapons under the blankets.

But the German trucks merely fled by without pausing, as if they found nothing unusual in the sight of three Afrika Korps trucks crossing the waste land by the side of the road.

The commando breathed again.

But their relief proved to be short-lived. From the moment they touched the Tobruk road there occurred a series of curious, disturbing events.

The first was a 'shufti kite' that seemed to flit out from the very wall of the escarpment itself. It was a light monoplane, the kind often used for aerial observation. All at once there was a roar of its engine above their heads, and their scrub-bearded, dirty faces lifted up in suspicion to watch it.

It seemed to float over them, completely encircling their three speeding vehicles; it was only a few hundred feet above their heads, and they could see the black dot of the pilot's head as he peered down at them. Twice he circled the tiny convoy, then abruptly the plane seemed to snatch away and disappear in the growing dusk towards El Adem airfield.

At least one member of the commando thought. 'They've got our number! That plane was waiting for us!'

Now they were moving towards the road block in the perimeter defences. Because of the plane the commando had little doubts as to the reception they would receive there. They took hold of their weapons and fingered safety-catches; if it came to a fight, they would tear their way through into Tobruk, they thought grimly.

The road block. In the leading truck Captain Bray, in the guise of a German officer, had his forged documents ready. He began to lean out of the truck, staring ahead. They could see the rusty, hanging, barbed-wire defences that marked the perimeter. A group of men stood by the opening where the road ran through. On either side were sandbagged defence posts.

The men were Italians. As the trucks came up, slowing a little, the perimeter guards stood aside and cheerfully waved them on. So Bray's driver, Wilenski, accelerated and began to go through. The tenseness was upon all the men now. They were watching the sandbagged defence posts. This was too easy, suspiciously so, entering Tobruk without so much as an examination of their papers. They watched the sandbagged enclosures and waited for machine-guns to open up on them. None did.

All three trucks swept into the gap in the wire. The

Italians waved and called greetings. Remembering their part, the Palestinians responded as Germans were expected to reply to their gallant allies. They shouted insults— '*Schweinhund!*' and other Germanic expressions of esteem for Mussolini's brave followers.

And it worked. Nobody tried to stop them. All at once they were through, they had penetrated Tobruk's outer defences. The tension drained away for a moment, exhilaration sweeping over the commando. Even the feeling that they were in a race against time momentarily left them.

Then they hit a German vehicle. A fast-moving column of transport approached them, heading out towards Alamein. There was a crash and the middle 3-tonner seemed to bounce and nearly go off the road. A German vehicle had smacked it a glancing blow. Graham Taylor thought it was a German truck; Weizmann, the Palestinian, swore it was a German staff car, containing a highly-decorated German major.

Nobody stopped to make sure. The 3-tonners belted a little bit faster on the road to Tobruk. Looking back, they saw the line of vehicles slow, as if halting around something hit. The commandos heard shouts in German—and shouted back. Then the convoy began to pull away again. Another bad moment had passed.

They were moving amid a fair stream of traffic now, so close to Tobruk. Light transport was overtaking them, so that at last they had a feeling they were in the midst of the enemy. On either side of them, too, were tented camps— lines of big tents that had probably been occupied by Allied troops only a few weeks before, including a red-crossed hospital camp. And everywhere Germans and Italians trudged alongside the road, mess tins swinging, as if they had just returned from their evening meal. Some of them looked up and stared with interest at the wild-looking 'prisoners' covered by the 'German' guards' German rifles.

Then three motor-cyclists appeared, pulling suddenly out from among the lines of tents. Two were German combinations, looking odd to British eyes with their sidecars on

the 'wrong' side of their machines, and the third a solo.
The motor-cyclists came up behind the rear truck and held
their position there for minutes on end. The 'P.O.W.s'
found themselves staring into the goggled eyes of German
military police. They felt uneasy. The motor-cyclists
appeared to be very interested in them.

Then all three began to pull alongside the Chevs. They
seemed still to be watching the prisoners, and in the rear
truck they felt pretty sure their ruse had been detected.

Major Campbell was sitting up against the tail-board.
He moved to screen the commando nearest to him and
said, softly, 'Get your gun, Glynn. I think the game's up.'

Sixteen-stone Private Glynn had his tommy-gun ready
under the blanket. The safety-catch was off, and he was
trigger-happy at the moment. The slightest untoward
move on the part of the German military police and he
was going to jump into action.

And then the motor-cyclists drew away and disappeared
ahead of the 3-tonners in the direction of Tobruk town.

Before they had time to get over their shock, another event
upset them, at least the men in the rear truck. They found
their attention suddenly absorbed by the conduct of one of
their own commando. He was a big, unimaginative
Guardsman; he had suddenly decided that he wanted to
relieve himself, so accordingly he stood up and did it over
the side of the speeding truck.

A horrified German-uniformed Langton watched in agony
and tried to think of conduct appropriate on such an occasion from a German guard. It was growing dark, true,
but they were running through the tented area and there
were lots of enemy soldiers about. Some were watching
the Guardsman, who stared stolidly back.

Then that, too, was over. The Guardsman adjusted himself, sat down and appeared blissfully ignorant of the agony
he had brought upon his comrades. The ride went on.

They passed a camp and a Verey light went up. There
seemed no reason for a Verey light to be fired behind a
tented camp and their eyes followed the curving, coloured

flare with immediate distrust and speculation. The trucks trundled on. Another Verey light soared aloft from behind another camp. Then another lifted and shed its brilliance in the gathering darkness.

The commando stirred uneasily. Someone growled, 'Looks as if someone's charting our progress into Tobruk.' Now they watched the ascending lights with foreboding. They had got through the perimeter defences with ease—was it because they were being led into a trap? First the shufti kite, then the begoggled military police . . . now the Verey lights which were being shot skywards for no reason apparent to the commando.

But nothing happened. There were no shots from the gathering night, no sudden cries to them to halt. The three trucks with their eighty commandos rolled steadily on to the end of their journey—gallant vehicles still running smoothly after more than eighteen hundred miles over some of the worst country in the world—a distance, as had been pointed out to the men, greater than from London to Warsaw.

They were almost into Tobruk town itself. They began to descend the second escarpment, crawling down the very steep roadway. To their right, they knew, would be El Gobi airfield. Intelligence said there would be Stukas based there. Stukas. . . . Nasty things for a thin line of earth-bound defenders to counter. . . .

Haselden suddenly spoke. He was in the back of a truck with others of his men. He nodded to where a high rock face loomed out of the near-darkness close by the road. They heard him say, 'That's the bomb-proof oil-storage depot we must destroy later to-night.'

Then the trucks went past it, leaving their most important target behind. Graham Taylor swore, 'We could have destroyed them as we passed!' They were so close. A few hand-grenades might even have done the trick. But the plan now demanded anonymity to their presence; they had to establish a bridgehead to bring in invasion troops, and *then* fight their way back to destroy the petrol dump.

At this moment, everyone knew that Haselden's original plan would have been successful. Haselden *could* have destroyed the dump, just as he had told G.H.Q., and probably got away with his men quite safely afterwards.

The leading truck seemed to be faltering. Palestinian drivers craned forward in their cabs, staring anxiously at Captain Bray's Chev, in front. It was halting. Something was wrong.

All the trucks stopped. Lanark got down and ran ahead into the darkness. Bray and a Palestinian were out of sight up the road. The blankets were off the men's knees now, guns up and ready, pointing in all directions into the night.

They could hear German being spoken. Then all the Palestinians got down and huddled round their officers. Plainly something was seriously wrong. Langton descended, too, and joined them. His German was bad and he understood only very imperfectly the cause of the consternation.

Someone had built a fence along the right-hand side of the road where no fence had ever been during the British occupation of Tobruk. The trouble was that the fence ran right across a side turning which the commando would have to follow in order to reach Mersa umm esc Sciausc— the bridgehead they were to capture.

Bray and some of the Palestinians went forward, scouting up the road. As Langton afterwards explained, he felt he had to contribute something to the moment, so he said, '*Jawohl, Jawohl,*' several times. Lanark's voice shot back in English, 'Shut up, you bloody fool!' Nerves were strained. Langton climbed back to his post covering the 'P.O.W.s.'

Then all at once the Palestinians and Bray were back. They were climbing into their cabs again. A feeling of relief swept over them. The scouting party had discovered that the fence ended a few hundred yards ahead, and a new track had been made south of Tobruk harbour.

The vehicles began to move forward, crawling in bottom gear behind each other.

The time was a little after nine. They were behind schedule, but not much behind, after all.

The long fence meant that they had to drive to within a few yards of the first buildings of Tobruk town itself. Plenty of enemy soldiers were moving about, mostly drifting into the town. Then they left the main road.

Bray's truck swung right on to a rough track, barely seen because now it was almost completely night. The others rounded the end of the fence, changing down with a noise that seemed shattering in the night. Then they began to trundle the last few hundred yards towards their objective.

They were almost home. The tension began to flow away; exhilaration took its place. Blankets were off and weapons held ready, though still down and out of sight. They kept passing groups of Italian soldiers, apparently taking an evening stroll, and the light was still not too bad because they recognized the party for British soldiers and shouted, '*Prizione?*'

At which everyone chorused in fluent Italian, '*Sì, sì.*'

So the Italians gaily cried, '*Viva Duce!*' and British razzberries topped the tribute. In fact, the atmosphere was highly harmonious.

The trucks bumped along in the dark for about ten minutes or quarter of an hour. Tobruk town lay north and west of the harbour, and they were running along the south shore. They were within yards of the sea—very near to Mersa umm esc Sciausc, their intended bridgehead.

They were almost there when suddenly there was a harsh challenge from ahead. A German sentry was there, rifle up. The trucks halted. There was no gaiety aboard now. An officer descended and walked into the darkness. They waited, tensed and vigilant, staring into the night around them. Silence for a few minutes.

Then the officer came walking back. He was carrying a German rifle. He handed it up, saying, 'Hang on to this. He won't need this where he's gone.' Then he climbed into his truck, and they bumped on a further five hundred yards.

Then, for the last time, the trucks stopped. They were there, at journey's end.

There were few orders and almost no talking. Everyone knew what to do. The men began to get down from their vehicles; equipment was handed out to them. Everything was done deliberately, without fuss or excitement. They fitted on their equipment as if they were about to go on parade on an English barrack square. No one hurried.

Now it was night. They had found their way to their destination right at the very last minute. But though there was no moon, there was the faintest glow of light reflecting from the sea, so that the rugged terrain about them was dimly silhouetted against the sky.

They realized that they were in some depression, perhaps part of a wadi that would terminate in the sea. North of them they could see the outline of a few huts near to what must be a cliff edge. They knew all about those huts. John Haselden's briefcase had been full of aerial photographs, which had clearly shown enemy gun positions east and west of the little inlet, and huts used probably as administration centres by the coastal defence battery.

Major Campbell was refusing aid with his equipment. He was terribly weak, but the London Scot had made the desert journey and he was going to play his part in the forthcoming drama, too. He began to pull out his party, calling softly to them in the darkness. They grouped to one side. Their job was to destroy two big guns which aerial photographs had shown to be on the east shore of Sciausc Bay and then clean up all opposition, including more big guns at a place once well known to British Tommies in Tobruk, called Brighton Rest Camp, two or three miles further east.

Haselden saw the burly figure of Tom Langton in the darkness. Langton, Harrison and Barlow were getting out of their German uniforms and equipment pretty quickly. Perhaps at the last second they were realizing how much they disliked the disguise, which would have brought them short shrift from the enemy if captured in their German clothing.

The Irish Guards officer felt his arm gripped, then heard Colonel Haselden's voice. 'Tom, I want you to go with

Colin's party. He's in a bad way, but he won't give in. If you find his strength gives out, take over.'

That made Langton straighten and start to do some calculating. His rôle had been a simple one until this moment. He had been deputed to help signal in the M.T.B.s and be on the beachhead to receive the landing force when their craft nosed into the little bay. He decided there was time to do both jobs—to help clear the east side of Sciausc Bay with Campbell's party, and then return to his position on the promontory.

He was turning. Campbell was already moving away across the wadi with his silent-treading, shadowy-formed party of commandos.

Then a gun fired somewhere in Tobruk.

There were three evenly-spaced shots, and they came from a biggish gun. In the darkness everyone stood tensed and waiting. Then someone—Bray or Lanark—spoke from the blackness.

'That's the air raid warning.'

XIV

FROM somewhere along the coast they began to hear the sharp blast of whistles and the shouts of N.C.O.s as the enemy ack-ack defences were manned. A light stabbed uncertainly into the sky over the sea, flickered, faded, then leapt into brilliant white strength. Other search-lights swung from across the harbour to join the first.

Distantly they head the thrum of aircraft engines. The R.A.F. were on time—the diversionary raid was beginning. It was exactly nine-thirty. Haselden's commando had reached their objective exactly at the second planned weeks before, eighteen hundred miles back along their desert journey.

Now Campbell's party slid away across the rocky wadi. Colonel Haselden began to climb on to the higher ground of a promontory to the west of Sciausc Bay. His men followed, not making a sound in their thick rubber-soled commando boots. The artillery officers, Barlow and Poynton, with their gunners, were with Haselden's party. They were not going to be left out of the next hour's events.

Now there was light as the coned searchlights began to swing more directly overhead. Too much light, some of the men began to feel. Then a flare burst over the target area, adding almost distressingly to the lightness across the bay. West of their position they heard a bellowed order that was drowned in the sound of a heavy ack-ack gun firing. Almost instantly other guns ringing Tobruk Harbour hurled their shells towards the steadily droning Wellington bomber. All at once the commando found itself in a world of raging sound.

But that was good; it would cover their movements.

Down below, Captain Trollope and his signals section,

including the two sailor-capped ratings, stood by the trucks that were soon to be destroyed. The R.A.F. pilot, Scott, was clambering along the promontory lugging an Aldis lamp—his was to be the loneliest, perhaps most nerve-racking job of all, just standing . . . waiting . . . and eventually signalling.

When they were all on top of the headland, the sea showing around them in the reflecting light from the moving, seeking searchlights, Graham Taylor, in command of west side operations, gave his orders.

'Form a line across the headland. Then lie down. Watch the skyline and don't let anyone pass. Don't fire, not until you receive orders from Colonel Haselden or myself.' For even though big guns barked, their sound was distant, expected and reassuring; but a rifle shot would be disturbing, warning.

The men strung out and went down on their stomachs, rifles, tommy-guns, even Bren-guns cuddling to them. The men had been allowed to bring any weapon they chose, the one with which they felt happiest. Then they waited, eyes watching the ragged skyline ahead.

They saw the flitting shapes of a party of officers go on towards a squat rectangle of blackness—the Italian house, as it had been marked on their maps.

No light came from the place. There was no sound from within. But there was no hesitation, no 'waiting to make sure'. This was a commando raid.

John Hasleden turned a door handle and walked into a candle-lit, bare-looking room. He went in without haste or bother, as if he were entering a room of his lovely white house on the Nile at El Minya. And for a second no alarm was felt by the occupants.

Three men were at a table. Italians. Blue-chinned and with highlights where the candlelight glistened on sweat-greased faces. One turned and looked towards the door-way, eyes heavy with boredom and the demands of frus-trated sleep. An N.C.O.

He saw an officer advancing across the room towards him.

Sleep flew from his eyes. He began to rise, began to salute. Then, and only then, did he notice the others following on Haselden's heels.

First, Graham Taylor. Then Captain Bray and Lieutenant Lanark in their German uniforms. And behind the officers big, grim S.S.M. Swinburn . . . and others.

A bewildered N.C.O. asked, ' *Tedesci* ?'—Germans? But his companions were beginning to scream now, screaming with the certainty of death before them. They had seen the pistol in Haselden's hand. They understood.

This was a raid by the dreaded, ferocious-fighting British commandos, about whom they had been warned. The shock of what it meant appeared to turn them crazy. For it seemed impossible to believe what their eyes saw now— here they were, three hundred miles from the fighting line, yet now they found themselves in deadly danger. It must have seemed somehow unfair to the bewildered, terrified Italians.

They grovelled abjectly, hands thrust out in supplication for mercy. They cried for their mothers and begged for their lives in the names of their wives and children.

They were thrust against a wall. Sharp questions in Italian were shot at them by Haselden and Bray. How many coast defence guns were on the headland? How many gunners manned them? Where were they now? And where were the telephone wires that provided communication between this part of the coast and Tobruk H.Q. itself?

More planes were droning overhead. More flares were descending. Bombs were falling little more than half a mile away in Tobruk town itself. Around them ack-ack guns erupted flame and noisily spat their deadly missiles into the night sky. The rolling barrage of sound was almost continuous.

Outside the men lay and waited and watched spouts of flame greet every falling bomb across the light-laddered water of the harbour. Their leaders seemed a long time inside the house. Then the door opened; they saw Swinburn come out. Some commandos were taken inside—to the Italians. The Italian N.C.O. was brought out. He had been so incoherent with terror that he had hardly been able to answer his terrifying, begrimed and bearded interrogators.

But he had said there were about fifty gunners on the site, with only four sentries guarding the coastal defence gun position. . . . More sentries? None of the commando had seen any sight of them.

The Italian said there were four main huts housing the gunners, and he agreed to show the commando party where the gun position command-post was. He did not know where the telephone cables ran but said he would help to try to find them.

Graham Taylor had ordered a commando corporal to tie the Italian N.C.O. to his, the corporal's wrist. Then it was they all filed out of the Italian house except for Haselden, who had decided to make the place his headquarters and was already searching through a pile of signals for helpful information.

A runner was sent down to tell Captain Gibson to come to the house and establish a first-aid post there; Captain Trollope and his signals staff were to come up with their equipment in one truck.

Taylor came across to the line of silent, watchful commandos, dimly seen in the uncertain light. He told them to get to their feet and prepare to advance. No one must be allowed to escape from the promontory to give warning beyond. But they knew their drill from previous rehearsals.

Taylor now went some distance ahead of his commando party. There was a lull in the firing, as momentarily all planes were out of range. Almost it was quiet, almost it was completely dark again as they moved noiselessly over the hard ground. Behind the lieutenant were the sergeant-major and two London Scottish privates, MacKay and Allardyce—Graham Taylor's invariable 'bodyguard'. David Sillito and the New Zealander, MacDonald, advanced with their sections. Barlow was over on the right, walking like a man out duck-shooting, and John Poynton with his four coast defence gunners was on the left flank. Bray, Lanark and the Palestinians were sliding off on some private marauding expedition.

Nothing happened for some minutes. The advance was made slow because of the absence of light and the need for silence and caution. It was time another plane came in. One was heard distantly out to sea. And distantly they heard enemy N.C.O.s' whistles as breech blocks slammed shut on fresh-loaded ack-ack rounds. But for the moment, silence.

Then—disaster. Or something suggesting disaster.

The Italian N.C.O. suddenly ran away. The commando corporal after all hadn't tied the man to his wrist, but had been holding him. The Italian saw his chance and took it. He jerked out of the corporal's grasp and fled like the wind. Sergeant-Major Swinburn got him. The man screamed as the giant S.S.M's bayonet went in, and then he was quiet.

But someone had fired at him, and the shot rang echoingly startlingly loud, to be heard by anyone on the silent promontory. Surprise was over.

The commando party surged forward quickly now. The thing was to get done what had to be done, and do it swiftly, to make up for the lost element of surprise. . . .

The line must have buckled in the dark. Someone saw a form ahead and fired. Then they found they had sustained their first casualty—Trooper McCall, an old Regular, was lying on the ground, wounded. He must somehow have got ahead of his companions.

And that was the second rifle shot to betray them. Taylor suddenly found himself running against some sandbag walls. They had reached the coast defence guns covering the entrance to Tobruk harbour. The walls were about five feet high, with a single narrow entrance.

Taylor led the way inside, his revolver out and ready. It was nerve-racking. Camouflage netting hung low across the pit. There were shadowy recesses which might contain ammunition—or men. And the netting caught the stooped Taylor round the buckles of the small pack on his back. For an agonizing half-minute he was hung up and had to be freed, and all the time he was caught they were expecting trouble.

But none came. No one was guarding the guns. It was astonishing—it was Italian.

They got through the gun pits. There were two guns, something like 25-pounders, John Poynton afterwards discovered. Near to them they found further sandbagging, this time around two searchlights. It was puzzling to know why they were not manned during an air raid, but there was still no sign of the enemy.

A small concrete hut loomed up. It looked like a strong-point, perhaps a sentry post. There was only one way to find out. Graham Taylor kicked open the door. He had a torch in his hand. Two rifles fired from within. Graham Taylor felt the shock as a bullet travelled right through his body; a second tugged at his stocking, tearing it and scratching his leg.

Allardyce and MacKay, his faithful followers, grabbed their leader and dragged him away. Sergeant-Major Swinburn swung his arm. A grenade hurtled into the concrete strong-point. More followed. Allardyce contributed. The sudden screaming of the two Italian sentries was lost in a succession of explosions.

The line surged on. Graham Taylor, sweating terribly but conscious, was helped to a little hut. There was a seat inside it, and they left him there. He felt good enough to look around in the hope of seeing some worthwhile souvenir—a pair of field-glasses, for instance. But there was only a Chianti bottle—empty. He had to sit and wait, out of the fight.

The commandos were moving without bother to hide their approach now. Around a searchlight-illuminated Tobruk harbour, guns roared, while mighty bombs crumped into the town already bombed almost out of existence by many air fleets. Bigger fires were raging now, reflecting redly across the water to the eyes of the grim commandos.

David Sillito had taken command. They were running on to huts built over shallow holes in the ground. The commandos tossed grenades in as they swiftly passed, or sprayed inside with tommy-gun bullets. There were men in them, men who had slept through all the noise of the night until then. Sometimes the commandos heard a scream, but that always brought another grenade and then there was silence.

On the east side of the promontory suddenly they came across a big hut. Sillito kicked open the door, just as Graham Taylor had done, taking the risk upon himself. He began to hurl grenades inside. He was thinking of Graham Taylor then and shouted for more grenades and threw them in. It was awful but it had to be done. The hut was packed with men, Italian gunners. Eight grenades went in, exploding. Then the commandos leapt inside, some with torches that lit up the carnage, others with tommy-guns chattering in the smoke-filled, echoing bunkhouse. Half naked Italians were clawing themselves out of their double-tiered beds. They were shouting, screaming, praying for mercy. It was a horrible, nightmare awakening. Others were already dead. When it was over they thought there were at least sixty killed inside that one hut alone.

Everywhere now on the headland the enemy was being routed. John Poynton with his gunners and some commandos had found a few small huts on the west side of the promontory. They went in, Poynton using a German rifle that had been presented to him by a Palestinian when the L.R.D.G. inadvertently went off with the gunnery officer's precious tommy-gun. About twenty Italians were killed. The Italian N.C.O's estimate of local troop concentrations was widely out. More Italians were running for their lives, clambering down to caves or among the rocks close by the sea around the tip of the promontory.

MacDonald's troop found some underground shelters. Sergeant O'Neill made a quick recce, found some ventilators and heard uneasy Italian voices below. He began to drop grenades through the ventilators. The rest of his men followed suit. About a dozen were rolled into each shelter. The screaming lasted for only a few seconds, and there was no need for the men to go into the huts with their torches and tommy-guns.

For another half-hour there was intermittent firing all across the headland. The N.C.O.s were finding terrified Italians, hiding up among the rocks, seeking a mercy that could not be given them.

And then all at once there was no opposition. It was surprising, in some way disconcerting. It had been too easy. They had expected a tougher resistance, a bloodier fight, but all in a matter of minutes they had cleared the far shore of Sciausc Bay. It meant that a bridgehead had been secured and that just outside Tobruk harbour.

It was unbelievable. The commandos stood staring suspiciously into a night that was coldly white from the searchlight beams, a night that seemed to shake with the thunder of the exploding bombs and the roar of defending guns. An incredible night.

But in time it dawned on them that things *were* as they seemed. They had really captured the promontory. There had been no death-trap for them in Tobruk, no hidden, waiting opposition to rout them. There had not even been sentries to watch out for them. And now a British force held ground in the vital Tobruk area for the first time since its fall four months before.

Someone came to Graham Taylor, sitting alone in the little wooden hut. They reported, 'We're all right at this side. We've cleared the place of the enemy.'

Graham Taylor looked at his watch in the light that came through the open doorway. It was just midnight. He called to Sergeant-Major Swinburn. ' Send up the success signal,' he ordered, handing over the Verey pistol he carried.

The tall sergeant-major went out. On the end of the promontory Pilot-Officer Scott saw the curving simultaneous red-and-green lights that said the west shore of Sciausc Bay was in British hands. His eyes turned eastward, along the darkened coast. When Campbell's signal went up, Scott would go into action. A runner had joined him on the lonely headland.   The two stood together in the darkness, tensely waiting.   Out at sea, they were thinking, silent-running M.T.B.s were closing in on the harbour; when they saw his flashing Aldis lamp they would steer in for Sciausc Bay.   But for the moment the Aldis lamp was not being used.   They were waiting on Campbell's party now.

Time passed.   Graham Taylor was helped to the first-aid post, where in candlelight he received attention from Captain Gibson.   By a miracle, it seemed, the bullet had passed through Graham Taylor's body without touching any ribs in the process.   But his lung was pierced, and that was serious enough.   Before morphine sent him to sleep, he realized that five other beds in the first-aid room were occupied by wounded.   Most had been shot by their own comrades—an inevitable accompaniment to a swift foray such as this.

Colonel Haselden was sitting behind a trestle table, receiving reports as runners came in, giving orders and co-ordinating operations, of necessity somewhat obscure because of the darkness.   Captain Trollope with his signals section and the two ratings were ensconced in a corner.

Bray and Lanark, with their S.I.G. followers, had cleared several huts in a small operation of their own.   This was right at the beginning of the assault across the promontory. Wilenski and Weismann of the S.I.G., with two commandos, had then been detailed to move inland a distance to hold back any attack from the direction.

They had found themselves among four ack-ack guns with dark forms running up as if to man them.   The four commandos opened fire at once.   The Italian gunners fled, but then came back with Schmeissers.   Over a period of several hours the quartet held the guns and drove off four resolute attacks designed to recapture them.   In time, though, it began to seem as though the Italians were now more concerned about escaping from the vicinity of the promontory than with capturing guns; things were unpleasantly hot for any enemy found in the vicinity of Sciausc Bay that night.

When opportunity presented itself the ack-ack guns were

each in turn destroyed. The commandos rolled grenades
into the barrels—then ran.

John Poynton, who was to have manned the coast defence
guns captured on the promontory, found himself under fire.
With his four gunners—big, resolute Lance-Bombardier
Stanton, Gunners Fairbairn, MacFarlane and Schyberg—
he had routed the enemy in dug-outs along the west coast
of the promonotory. But in the darkness the Italians kept
coming back, and the artillery officer found himself the
subject of harassing attacks.

Poynton reported back to Colonel Haselden; Haselden
ordered Poynton to seal off the tip of the promontory and
prevent a rear attack on his H.Q. in the Italian house. It
was quite an assignment, but Poynton settled down to hold
the coast defence guns all through the night. In between
times he managed to examine the guns: they were old, in
poor condition, and without sights; there appeared to be no
ammunition in the gunpits for them, either, and he abandoned any ideas he might have had of trying to man one
gun with his few gunners.

Time was passing. It was passing too quickly. In his H.Q.
John Haselden was beginning to worry. He called to David
Sillito—he was anxious about Major Campbell's party.
No signal had come from him, and it was now approaching
half-past one. By now a signal should have been received,
for the M.T.B. fleet would be offshore with their invasion
troops. The bombing still continued, with searchlights
and gunfire following the droning Wellingtons. But though
the pilots of 205 Group were careful to plant their big bombs
among the flames of Tobruk town, north of the harbour,
no longer now were they using flares.

Promptly at one o'clock, Sunday the 14th, the airmen
had stopped dropping flares. For by now the two destroyers,
Sikh and *Zulu*, should be closing in on the north shore to
land their marine commando, and would want a darkened
shoreline. Without the flares it seemed very dark on the

south shore around Mersa umm esc Sciausc. Dark and chilly, for now that the fighting was over the men shivered in their sweat-wetted shorts and shirts and they kept moving to keep warm.

Some of them went down on to the sandy beach of the little cove and walked about and even smoked a surreptitious cigarette. It seemed unreal, to be strolling about without hindrance right in the midst of the enemy. They looked out to sea, between the headlands that closed in on the entrance to the tiny harbour. Out there were the reinforcements. When they came there would be more action.

It would be a story to thrill the people back home, the commandos thought. Tobruk destroyed; Rommel hurt beyond all recovery on the eve of one of the mightiest battles in history. If they never had another night, at least they were satisfied with what they had done in the past four hours.

Their shadowy shapes drifted together on the dark headland. They wanted to get on with the job instead of hanging about.

But the signal from Campbell was late in coming. Far later than they had expected. The exhilaration after their swift victory began to ebb away in the coldness of the night during the long vigil. No longer were they interested in watching the pounding of the north shore by the procession of Wellingtons; in time because of their anxiety they scarcely noticed the air raid, or thought about their curious position on this isolated promontory in the midst of the enemy.

Major Campbell and his party had been gone for hours. When it reached one-fifteen the anxiety became alarm. The race against time had begun again. If no success signal was received very soon from Haselden's commando, the whole thing would be called off. The fleets of ships out at sea would be turned back to Alexandria.

And themselves? Their escape if there was no destroyer to pick them up? The commandos gave little thought to it, to their own safety. Their main, worrying concern now was —*what was holding back the success signal from Campbell's party?*

XV

ACTING-LEADING WREN Eva Porter knew there was something in the wind the moment she reported for duty in the Signals Distributing Office, H.Q. Alexandria, on September 13. As she took her place behind her typewriter she looked around.

The room was unusually crowded with officers. What surprised her was the Army 'brass' there—unusual to see Army officers in that particular office. There was something of an air of tension about the officers, too, and experienced as she now was, the tall, dark Wren from Grimsby knew there was a hazardous operation pending.

But she had her own problems—a boy in the *Coventry* and another in the Coding Room. Life could be hell for a poor Wren unable to make up her mind, she was thinking, slipping a stencil into her machine and beginning to tap out a message handed across by the Leading Hand of the Watch.

Then as the clock hands moved into the early hours of of the morning of the 14th, Acting-Leading Wren Eva Porter forgot her own problems. The excitement was growing hourly. Officers kept dashing into the room demanding to know if certain signals had been received. Others, including the brass, just hovered around and smoked and talked in desultory fashion, to be galvanized only when a message came through for stencilling and eventual distribution.

Their eyes were on the clock. They were watching the hands crawl round. Crawl? By half-past one they were beginning to think the hands were racing.

For they knew what Eva Porter did not know. That if no success signal was received from Colonel Haselden by two in the morning, the raid would be cancelled and the ships brought home.

Two o'clock .... The minute hand began to crawl towards the hour. Quarter to two and no message. Ten minutes to ... five to two. Four minutes to go. The cancellation message was all ready. Three minutes ... two minutes ...

At one minute to two the Leading Hand gave a signal to the Wren for typing. It consisted of one word. She began to tap it out in the prescribed way—N-I-G-G-E-R.

The officers were suddenly crowding around, suddenly jubilant. There was noise and excitement in the room, and officers grabbed their own copies of the signal as it was run off and dashed away with them.

'Nigger'. The codeword meaning success for Haselden— the bridgehead at Sciausc was now in British hands and the M.T.B.s could go in with their troops.

It had arrived with one minute to spare.

Tom Langton fired the success signal along the coast east of Sciausc Bay. It was late, just after one-fifteen, but in time, they were all sure. They were not to know of the delays taken in enciphering, transmission and deciphering of the message which had almost caused it to be too late at Alexandria.

Away on the darkened east-coastline, too, Major Campbell and his men were not to know of the jubliation in Haselden's H.Q. when someone first spotted their success signal—two green Verey lights simultaneously. The old exhilaration of victory again swept over the little knot of men at sight of those soaring lights. Around the Italian house, men thumped each other and shook hands, and then grasped their weapons more firmly as if anxious to use them again. Frowsty, bearded faces beamed upon each other with the relief at the passing of the tension.

David Sillito brought the news in to John Haselden. Haselden was delighted. Sillito saw him smile with pleasure and relief because the waiting was over, and yet the lieutenant had a feeling that Haselden was just a little surprised at the demonstrations of delight in the H.Q. .... as if in his heart the commando leader had never seriously doubted that success would attend their attack.

Haselden gave the word to Captain Trollope, standing before his big ship's radio transmitter. 'Send "Nigger",' he said. Then he went out to watch for the incoming M.T.B.s.

Major Campbell had been late, all the same, in despatching his success signal from the east shore. But then two unreckoned for events had happened to throw his calculations out.

The first was a minefield across the wadi. All at once in the darkness an alert sapper gave the warning—''ware minefield!'

It brought them all up with a jerk. They froze where they were in the darkness, not daring to move for a moment. The drill for mine detecting came into operation—the detachment of sappers with the party began to use their detection apparatus, clearing a path across the field.

It was a slow business, and it meant that the commando had to close into single file and follow on the heels of the sappers; they were easy targets for any enemy sentries on the prowl, a solid line of men like an island in a sea of mines, unable to move quickly, rendered helpless by the deadly unseen explosives all around them.

But seemingly there were no sentries, and in time the agony was over and a sweating, silently cursing commando found itself through the danger area. But time had raced away.

They began to move more quickly along the slope of the wadi now, when again they were halted, tensed and alert and staring all ways into the hostile darkness.

A rifle had fired somewhere ahead of them.

They waited. Nothing happened. The expected attack from the darkness never began. Now it was about midnight and so far they had achieved nothing.

Mike Roberts received an order from Major Campbell. 'Take your section and recce ahead. Whoever's there, get round them and drive them on to us.'

Mike Roberts went gladly away, followed by his silent-moving commandos. More waiting. They listened to the sound of the droning bombers, the roar of ack-ack guns, and watched the devastation across the harbour from them. *Time was going awfully fast.*

Then they were electrified to see a Verey light west of

them. Two reds simultaneously. Haselden was telling
them that he had succeeded. And they hadn't started!
Damn that minefield and rifle shot!

Tom Langton came up beside his leader. 'I'd like to
make a recce,' he said. 'I want to see if the beach is clear
where the M.T.B.s are to land.'

Major Campbell gave permission. In spite of his weak-
ness, he was bearing up well.

Langton went away, holding his tommy-gun ready for
action. He found himself walking on sand. Ahead of him
the sea washed in, and he could see the sheen of reflecting
light at times when the angle of the searchlights was right.

He walked right across the bay and encountered nobody.
The M.T.B.s could come in without opposition, he thought.
Then he looked at the shadowy headland to the east of the
inlet and thought, 'There might be guns there. They've
got to be cleared.' He was disturbed by the feeling of time
racing on, and he went back to Campbell without delay.

Mike Roberts returned at the same time. It was mystify-
ing. There was no enemy ahead, and no explanation for
the mysterious rifle shot. Langton said, 'The beach is open,
sir. I think that's our quickest way now.'

Major Campbell told him to lead the way, and now
they moved on swiftly to clean up the east coast section.

It was a ticklish, uncertain business, trying to find an
enemy before he found them; trying to dispose of him without making too much noise and so alerting the whole area.
They moved off in sections under their lieutenants, Murphy,
Roberts and Duffy, each exploring, each going in when
they contacted an enemy.

Mike Roberts found the first nest. It was a Spandau,
walled up among the rocks. Under cover of noise from the
ack-ack barrage, Roberts suddenly went running in before
the enemy could get their gun into action. He stormed
inside, tommy-gun chattering, his men racing up in support.
Within seconds there was no opposition and Roberts and
his section were continuing their deadly prowl among the
rocks above the unseen, beating waves of the open sea.

Next thing Roberts found was a radio station. He and his men stormed it with guns and grenades; a quick, vicious little fight, red flashes sparking the shadowy night, men crying and dying and their set disintegrating as a grenade erupted against it.

Now they moved more rapidly, anxious to mop up the area. Little groups of commandos kept running into each other, challenging, 'Who goes there?' And George Robey would answer back. Only, if he spoke in Italian he received a gun burst instantly.

Then Mike Duffy came striding through the night, his commando section at his heels. He saw Langton with Major Campbell and reported. 'I've found the gun positions, sir.' These were the big, sandbagged emplacements that had been photographed from the air and were thought to hold a coast defence battery. Now Mike Duffy reported, 'They're all empty and unused, sir.'

There was a commotion east of them, where Lieutenant Murphy's section was in action against some isolated Italian machine-gun post. But it was well east; they had advanced probably a mile or more along the rocky coast.

Langton was getting worried because he had to go back to the bay to start signalling, and he was to guide the landing parties in. He said, 'Shall we put up the success signal, sir?' Duffy's report was reassuring; no big guns remained to cover Sciausc Bay.

Major Campbell said, 'Yes, Tom. Send it up.'

It was then just after quarter-past one. Langton set off back to the east point to start his signalling. Major Campbell continued with his men to attack guns thought to be at Brighton Rest Camp.

Langton found it slow going, hurrying alone through the darkness. Far too slow. Sweating from the exertion and strain of keeping watch for the enemy, stumbling over ground far too rough for rapid travelling, Langton realized that he would never make the inlet in time to signal in Force C. That is, not if first he had to return to the Italian house and get his Aldis lamp.

There was nothing for it, he had to compromise. He had his torch with him. He decided to use that instead of the Aldis, though it was far less powerful and was white instead of the required red. Still, he had no alternative.

As he clambered into position on the east point he saw Scott's red light flashing on the west promontory. Langton had lost his watch on the journey up from Kufra. Now he was obliged to time his signals with Scott's flashing Aldis lamp. The signal—three long flashes every two minutes on a bearing N.E. and E. It had been due to start at 0130 hours; Scott at least had been on time, even if Langton was a little late.

Scott, lonely in the darkness for all the companionship of one runner, began his signalling immediately Campbell's Vereys curved into the sky. He seemed already to have been hours at his post; he had no idea of the time, and thought it must surely be close on dawn, though in fact daybreak was still over three hours away.

Scotty was wondering why he had volunteered for such folly. He simply could not understand these commandos who liked fighting on *land*. In future he would do his fighting from the comfort of a warm, cosy bomber. At that moment, cold and uneasy, isolated on the wind-swept point, Scotty would have welcomed the fiercest barrage of flak over an enemy target. Just to have a bomber around him, he kept thinking; something that he could manœuvre and fight back from and after the swift, neat operation of dropping its load, go speeding to base and a pleasant breakfast remote from the happenings of war. These commandos, he kept thinking, weren't human. They seemed to be enjoying their night foray. They seemed quite unconcerned about the day ahead. . . .

Some time after two o'clock, unease began to mount again. It was a night of alternating hopes and anxieties, they were beginning to realize. But the M.T.B.s should have been entering Sciausc Bay promptly at two, they knew, and as the minutes ticked by they began to fear the worst.

For some of them, the ones with imagination, there came

a spectre of doubt to disturb their minds. They had a momentary vision of M.T.B.s lost in the dark wide sea beyond the high, rocky entrance to the bay. After all, it seemed incredible that boats could find such a tiny landfall in the midst of such blackness. The unease kept returning, and with it the thought: 'We've captured this bridgehead, but perhaps nothing will come through.' When daylight came they might still be standing there, a target for a vastly more powerful enemy, with all ways of escape cut off from them. Destroyers? They shrugged away the thought that perhaps the destroyers wouldn't be able to get through to take them off.

And in that moment many of them were remembering the huts filled with Italian dead, the corpses that littered the headland. If they were trapped here at Sciausc, they could expect little mercy from the enemy.

It was two-thirty. Force C was half an hour late. By now a submarine would have surfaced opposite Mersa Mreira, on the north coast beyond Tobruk harbour; three folbotists would long ago have paddled shorewards, two to position themselves on high ground on either side of Mreira Bay, one in his canoe in the centre of the little harbour. It would be eerie, agonizing work, paddling in towards a shore occupied by an enemy. . . .

Colonel Haselden was walking about now, restless because the plan was going wrong. His patrols were continually going out, making sure there was no enemy in the vicinity and they could see the Arab-head-dressed colonel striding from place to place, as if he could no longer sit behind the trestle table in the H.Q. and receive reports. Sometimes he was seen walking about carrying his precious briefcase. It was incongruous, the combination of briefcase and Arab head-dress under those circumstances. And sometimes he went down to the sandy beach and stared out to sea, or looked up at Scott signalling—Langton was out of sight because of the curving shoreline.

Time left half-past two and became something to three. No M.T.B.s came in. The plan had gone wrong again. Haselden went back to his H.Q.

XVI

FOR Force C, the fun began immediately it grew dark. Until then they had been keeping good stations, in two neat columns containing sixteen M.T.B.s and three Fairmiles.

But with darkness, and their change of course for Tobruk, it became necessary to head for land at high speed—and M.T.B.s can really travel when required. Suddenly they had to bring their speed up from eighteen knots to about thirty knots, and still keep stations in the darkness.

The manœuvre was only partially successful. One column snatched away, accelerating incautiously, so that the units were lost to each other within seconds. The other column successfully brought its main engines on while keeping in steady line astern and made good progress towards Tobruk harbour. With half the force lost in the darkness the landing operation was jeopardized from the start.

Force C had to go into Mersa umm esc Sciausc at 0200 hours, and one column of M.T.B.s made land about on time. As they raced in towards the shore, they were in a blackness that was complete and profound except directly ahead, where flames followed explosions and lit tall columns of smoke in a red glow over Tobruk town.

The raid was on. Overhead, bombers droned in steady procession on to their target, and the crump-crump of their bombs—the biggest ever dropped in a Middle East raid—came clearly to the ears of the approaching Force C. Tobruk was being well and truly smashed, this night, and they could see the impotence of the weaving columns of light that tried to pick out the Wellingtons, and almost they could feel the angry frustration of ack-ack gunners shooting their shells and tracer at a seemingly unperturbed enemy. Tobruk was certainly putting on a first-class firework display.

But south of the harbour, where Sciausc Bay would be, was silent and in blackness. Eyes stared ahead, looking for a guiding signal to mark the harbour entrance. They saw none.

And the wireless operators, headphones on and listening all the time, sat without reporting any success signal from Haselden's commando. It was disturbing. Their orders were not to go in unless they had received the success signal, 'Nigger'. And if they didn't receive it by two o'clock, they were to expect a signal from Alexandria calling the whole show off.

The M.T.B.s gathered offshore in the darkness, running on silent engines, weaving close up and down the coastline. It was well past two o'clock. Some of the M.T.B. stragglers began to come up, too.

There was some mist drifting near to the land. It was nothing much, but it might have been more obscuring than at first they thought. And as for non-receipt of radio signals, M.T.B.s' sets were notoriously unreliable; they were never powerful enough, and always got wet in the little ships.

As time went swiftly by, with still no signal, tension aboard the M.T.B.s grew proportionately. All the men were ready to take to the assault craft, and they were tired of the delay and wanted only the action for which they had been trained.

Some of the M.T.B.s went exploring, to make sure they were not out in their calculations. One found itself within fifty yards of the coast in a bay which they identified as Mersa Biad, next to Mersa Sciausc; there were no lights ashore, no movement—they could have landed with ease. But that wasn't in the programme, and it would do no one any good to find themselves being assailed in the darkness by Haselden's men. They pulled out and circled again. It was exasperating, but that was all they could do—keep on waiting and hoping for a signal.

The one consoling feature was the fact that the enemy seemed blissfully oblivious of their presence. All lights were following the aircraft; all attention, seemingly, was upon the Wellington bombers. In the time they were there they could have landed regiments . . . it was so dark and quiet outside Mersa umm esc Sciausc. Even the sea was placid enough at this point.

Two Italian destroyers sped through the night towards Tobruk. The commanding officers were Captain Mickle-thwait and Commander White.

Parties had begun work immediately at sunset on Saturday night, painting both ships an overall grey. The *Sikh* had had the black top of her foremast funnel painted out, and both 'Tribal' destroyers had had their decks desecrated with the red and white diagonal stripes that were the Italian identification signal.

For both destroyers had work to do once they had landed their marine commando. *Sikh* and *Zulu* would then go round to Tobruk harbour proper, smash their way through the boom defences, and then run amok among the shipping inside.

That done, the two 'Tribals' would take up berths allocated in the planning, they would list ship to 15 degrees (which was quite a lot and would give the appearance of ships sinking), then they would make smoke and light fires aft on the upper deck. Enemy aircraft not properly briefed would mistake them for Italian destroyers sinking at their moorings, would leave them alone and probably paste other ships.

That was the planning. But neither Captain Mickle-thwait nor Commander White could have been very optimistic about their chances of survival; for during planning they had been issued with a mine chart showing the entrance to Tobruk harbour. It was probably the most dismal picture any captain loving his ship could see. It was a mass of mines—mines lavishly laid by Germans, aided by more mines dropped by our own Navy and R.A.F.

True, Intelligence had got hold of something which they said confidently was a plan of the Italian-swept channel, but it was nothing to get two ships' commanders over-enthusiastic.

All they could see were about three hundred mines over which their precious vessels would have to pass before getting in. If *Sikh* and *Zulu* made that run in safety, then a miracle would have happened.

Colonel Unwin was trying to satisfy some irreconcilable problems, too. At the last minute the marine commander had found himself hoisted with an astonishing collection of bods who had briskly come aboard at Alexandria. Unwin was not sure what they were all about. The ones with flourishing moustaches were R.A.F., of course, and were blithely asking to go ashore at Tobruk so as to pinch a piece of enemy radar. It was possibly the same piece that Lloyd Owen intended to pinch.

Another bod was a naval lieutenant. He was a safe-breaker.

The problem was that all had to be taken ashore, and Unwin just hadn't the boats for the extra passengers. It was a problem which could only be deferred.

When they were seventy miles off shore, the destroyers began to see the effects of the air raid on Tobruk. As they grew nearer the pyrotechnic display improved; they found themselves under a lane of bombers sweeping in to the attack from the sea. Just before three in the morning, they saw what must have been a tremendous explosion ashore, as if some mighty ammunition dump had received a direct hit.

Tobruk seemed to be blazing fiercely, and drifting smoke was obscuring the coastline and made location of the landing beach difficult.

Dead on time, at exactly 0300 hours, Monday morning, both ships stopped about two miles off the unseen shore. With their bows to the beach they began to get out the boats—those 'bloody boot-boxes'. It should have taken twenty minutes, but it took forty.

It had been rehearsed over and over again, so that the crews were perfect in their drill. But it was extraordinarily difficult to perform in the pitch blackness.

The dumb lighters were aft on the upper deck, tucked into each other; the topmost ones had to be lifted out using the torpedo davits. The davits had to be trained inboard and the winch hove round by hand until the boats were clear of each other; then they were turned out and lowered into the water.

The trouble was that in the dark the man at the winch couldn't see the davits, and the man at the davits couldn't shout to the man at the winch because the whole thing had to be conducted in silence.

Nevertheless this ticklish part of the operation didn't go too badly. But on the *Sikh* a shackle broke and then the pantomime really began. The marines, stoically waiting below with all their weapons and equipment, kept getting whispers down to them. Frantic efforts were being made in the darkness to repair or replace the shackle. While this was being done, the buzz came round that one of the crew had got his hand jammed. Later it was said that he had lost a finger.

But in time all the boats were slung out, and the marines began to file up on deck to get into their landing craft. It was a disagreeable experience.

The submarine *Taku* might have signalled that conditions were good for a landing, but it was not as far as the boot-boxes were concerned. They were horrifying contraptions, quite useless in such a sea. And it was slapping about pretty nastily against the destroyers' sides, both of which were rolling heavily.

They got the first flight into the lighters, though no one ever knew how it was accomplished in such darkness, with the plyboard craft ducking and rolling and swinging away every few seconds.

Then the motorized craft had to creep round in the dark and pick up their tows. There were wild moments, when it seemed as if everybody would go in the drink, and there were savage curses for blankety boat builders who lived in Haifa. Yet in time all craft were in tow and the first assault flight was ready to depart.

There appeared to be no problem, so far as the Senior Naval Officer was concerned. He had received a relay from Alexandria at 0210—just the one word, 'Nigger'. True, Captain Micklethwait had been expecting it around midnight, and it had been disturbing, not receiving it until almost the moment when they were coming in to attack. But at last the success signal was received. Haselden had captured his precious bridgehead, and Force C should already be ashore now.

A curious feature, though, was that at 0145 a signal had been received from the submarine *Taku*, via Alexandria, saying 'Folbotists landed and found no one on beach.' But no signals could be seen from the shore. Only occasionally could a white light be seen, and that a mere intermitten glimmer which could hardly be called a guiding light.

Nevertheless, the show was on; Haselden's commando held a bridgehead in the vital area. Now it was the marines' turn, and they were bursting to storm ashore.

The order was given, the plunging, awkward craft wallowed away in the heaving night sea and were lost to sight within seconds. The first flight was away; there was complete darkness along the shore opposite. So far the landing had been undetected—the enemy was too concerned with the attackers upstairs, the marauding Wellington bombers.

At 0348 the marines were released for their shore run: *Sikh* and *Zulu* turned and steamed seaward at fifteen knots so as to be less easily detected if the enemy were alerted by the landing. At 0414 the destroyers came back to the coast again.

Then their wireless receivers brought a disturbing message. It was from Colonel Unwin. His power boat contained the only transmitting set with the marine landing force, and he was signalling back that his tow of boats was drifting helplessly at sea—his motor had broken down.

This was sobering news. It meant that the marine force was landing without its leader and there was no means of communicating with them.

It was disturbing.   The two big destroyers came slowly in
to about a mile off the beach—nearer than had been planned
but probably with the idea of saving time in meeting the
returning craft which were to take in the second flight of
marines.

About this time a very bright light was seen to flash on the
coast opposite.   The naval party watched it and decided that
it was a signal from a folbotist warning of strong opposition
ashore.

At 0500, fighting became apparent on the shore.   Aboard
the ships they saw mortar and machine-gun tracer fire.
After a few minutes it seemed to be moving eastwards.

And nowhere in the darkness could they see a sign of
returning assault craft.   The first flight of marines was being
attacked on shore and the second flight, staring helplessly
from the decks of the destroyers, armed to the teeth, were
unable to get across to help them.

XVII

Scott, sure now that they were hours behind time, continued to flash his lamp out to sea at the prescribed intervals. He was mildly worried because he could not see Tom Langton signalling from the east point, but decided that there would be a simple explanation for the omission—Langton must have positioned himself where his light would be screened.

He was cold and hungry, stiff from the wind that blew around him, and was trying not to think of what happened when a desperate plan failed.

Something moved. It was something faintly lighter than the dark shoreline opposite. For a second Scott ignored it. Then his incredulous eyes swung round to follow the movement; he found himself almost shouting, 'They're here! Thank God, at last they're here!'

An M.T.B. was in the harbour, pulling into the shadow of the high rock wall to the west of the cove. It moved without the slightest sound or disturbance of the water. It was unreal, uncanny. It was deliriously exciting.

And then a second M.T.B. found the entrance and came smoothly, sweetly into the bay.

Tom Langton caught the movement, too. He had a better idea of time than Scott, because someone had mentioned the time when the two green Verey lights went up. Somewhere around three, he was thinking—late but perhaps not critically late, after all.

But he had to go down to receive the M.T.B.s and that set a problem. How could he keep on signalling, and at the same time go down to greet the landing party? That was the result of the change of plan, because he hadn't had time to return for an Aldis lamp and at the same time get a runner. . . .

Langton compromised, as again he had to. He switched on his torch and allowed it to shine out to sea, wedging it among the rocks. Then he clambered on to the higher ground and began to grope his way round to the beach.

His tommy-gun and pack got in the way, and he was in a hurry, so he carefully put both into a sangar and clambered on. When he dropped down on to the sandy beach, he realized that two M.T.B.s were already in. To his relief he heard the strong New Zealand accent of MacDonald. Mac was already on the job.

For a little while he hung about, glad to feel contact with the outside world through the M.T.B.s and their reinforcements. There was an air of bustle about the beach, even though operations were shrouded in darkness. Men were leaping off the M.T.B.s—they seemed enormously high above their heads—and guns and equipment were being slung down to them.

Mac was moving from one M.T.B. to the other, giving orders, asking questions. He seemed to have the situation under control. Langton, reassured, started back up the rocks to his lonely post. When he reached the sangar he went inside.

He came out instantly. Someone had walked off with his tommy-gun and small pack.

He drew his revolver. It was an unpleasant feeling, to be alone there in the darkness and not know what eyes were watching him, what guns were training on him at that moment. For, one thing he knew—whoever had stumbled upon his gun in his brief absence had been no friend.

He walked suspiciously towards his blazing torch.

MacDonald was delighted with the reinforcements. A short, sturdy man was first off the M.T.B., announcing themselves in a north-country voice as Northumberland Fusiliers.

'Machine-guns,' said Mac with satisfaction. Just the job if trouble brewed up, as it would.

The ammunition cases seemed enormously heavy, coming over the side of the M.T.B., and Mac despatched a runner for the wireless truck. In a few minutes it came bumping down the wadi with its headlights on. It pulled round short of the sand, and the Fusiliers began a swift portage of their two Vickers machine-guns and cases of ammo from boat to truck. Mac and his section of commandos gave willing assistance. When the Fusiliers came within the rays of the headlights, they were seen to be neatly shaven, and looked very clean and smart. After weeks of non-washing, and with hairy faces all round, clean-shavenness looked somehow improper to the commandos.

Mac heard swearing on the M.T.B. nearest him. He called out, 'What's wrong?'

A voice said, 'We've piled the bloody thing on to the putty.'

'Can't you get off?'

A laconic voice, 'Don't you think we're trying, brother?'

He heard the powerful beat of M.T.B. engines as the skipper drove hard astern. The M.T.B. shook but stayed put. Mac walked aside so that he could look beyond for more incoming M.T.B.s. He felt cheerful. Two had found the harbour without difficulty; the others should all be crowding in within minutes. He decided to wait and welcome them.

He kept on waiting. He was down on the beach an awful long time. He was there long after the truck had ground its noisy way up the wadi, bearing the reinforcements—after all, only nine men including the tough little sergeant—and guns to positions of vantage up the hillside.

He heard conversation between the skippers of the two craft, and he thought one was attempting to tow the other off. Then he decided to report back to Haselden. It seemed to MacDonald that firing had broken out south and west of their positions—small-arms firing that was heard in the lulls between the bombing raids. He never saw the M.T.B. that finally left the harbour.

Pilot-Officer Scott watched it go out just as silently as it had entered. He was still signalling, perturbed again because of the lack of results. He knew the operation was again running well behind time.   And yet the night was still dark and silent—as silent, that is, as a night can be during an air raid.

Quite some time after the solitary M.T.B. had departed, Scott saw a solitary searchlight suddenly beam down from the sky and throw itself like a barrier across the entrance to Sciausc Bay.   The next second it seemed that every search-light suddenly abandoned pursuit of aerial targets and all in one movement began to search the sea.

It was as if someone inside Tobruk had suddenly signalled a warning: 'Forget the air raid.   We are being invaded from the sea.'

At about 0505 hours on Black Monday morning Operation Agreement became suddenly known to the enemy.   The tragedy was about to begin.

And it was about this time, too, that MacDonald's section ran into heavy enemy small-arms' fire west of their position at Sciausc Bay.   And that was the beginning of the end for Haselden's commando.

Captain Lloyd Owen tripped over an aerial stay in the dark and went flat on his face.   It was not the first time it had happened, and his language was getting stronger.

There was an edge to the Army words, too, because he was not altogether happy.   He was wanting to contact John Haselden before taking his patrol in through the perimeter, but his wireless operator only growled, 'Blast them, why don't they answer!'   Force B was not on the air.   Lloyd Owen found fears growing in his mind natural to the situation.   His biggest fear, finally resolving, was that Haselden had driven blindly into a trap.

Finally, as late as he dared, he gave the order, 'Pack up. Let's get moving.'

He was restless and wanting action again.   They had had a good supper, quite openly lighting a fire and sitting round it, though only fifteen miles from Tobruk, and now a warming tot of rum was rationed out.   It was quite cold now, with a bitter wind blowing, and the rum ration was welcome.

Then they got into their trucks and began to drive in line ahead towards the perimeter. It was dark—solidly, unrelievedly black all around them; so they switched on their headlights and drove openly through the night. Long ago the L.R.D.G. had learned that audacity is the first weapon of irregulars such as themselves.

They had expected to be at the perimeter soon after ten, but they found it awful going this black night down the escarpment at Sidi Rezegh, and they lost time and as they did so little feelings of panic began to well within them. The L.R.D.G. did not want to be late for their particular part in the night's programme, but above all they did not want to let Haselden's men down.

The escarpment seemed to be working against them. In the end they almost had to build a road down that rugged, rocky, almost precipitous cliff edge; there were moments when they thought their trucks were going over and they hung on like grim death, their hearts in their mouths. Only fools—and L.R.D.G.—would be so crazy as to try to get down an escarpment after dark.

But finally they reached more level ground. The bombers were giving Tobruk the works now, and they paused to watch the weaving searchlights and the speckle of bursting anti-aircraft fire. They saw, too, the eruption as bombs blasted into the town and started fires and caused explosions, Four-thousand-pound bombs were being used to-night, they had been told. It certainly sounded like it. To be in Tobruk must have been sheer hell that night.

There were lights on the plain before them, so Lloyd Owen drove to avoid them. He was steering by the stars, and the going was better and the headlights seemed brilliantly helpful.

Then, quite suddenly, Lloyd Owen saw concrete revealed in the glare of his headlights. He thought, 'A pillbox!' At the same instant he heard men shouting. So he shouted, too. He yelled to his driver, 'Step on it!' and they went through with a rush.

Behind him there was firing, a sudden, heavy crashing

burst that told him his men in the rear trucks were in action. Half a mile on in the darkness, Lloyd Owen told his driver to halt. They paused, ready with their guns, looking back, but could see nothing.

So Lloyd Owen got out of his truck and flashed a torch. He lived, so he decided to attract more attention. He began to shout. Either there were no Germans or Italians lurking near or they thought no enemy could be fool enough to kick up such a row, so Lloyd Owen continued to live.

Suddenly from the darkness came the voice of Sergeant Hutchins. There was more flashing of torches and shouting, and they got together. The L.R.D.G. were excelling themselves this night.

Lloyd Owen counted the trucks as they lurched up. When he found one was missing he made a check. Of course it had to be their wireless truck. Without wireless they were dumb and useless creatures, and they had to get it back whatever the risk. Again, in it were the codes and ciphers and those must not fall into the hands of the enemy.

Then men began to emerge from the darkness, very breathless. It was the crew of the wireless truck. They said their truck had been hit and they had been unable to start it. At once Lloyd Owen took ten men with tommy-guns and rifles back through the darkness towards the pillbox.

L.R.D.G. fighting was always somehow outrageous, completely divorced from what the drill books laid down. All too often, too, it held something ludicrous, something pantomimic in quality. This quality was certainly present that night.

Lloyd Owen was in a hurry. He continued of necessity to draw attention to themselves, to the presence of an enemy near to the Axis stronghold. He fired a Verey pistol to see what lay ahead. His men were flat while he did it. but he stood and peered around and tried to make out the abandoned truck. He thought he saw it, and they went scouting ahead. It turned out to be a derelict horse-drawn water cart. They did a lot of cursing, so Lloyd Owen ripped off with quite a number of Verey lights.

They were in the midst of the enemy, they knew that. After all they were within yards of where the brush had occurred, and the enemy must still be lurking around. Yet just nothing happened. No one opened up when the Verey lights curved through the sky. In Lloyd Owen's own words, the enemy seemed remarkably uninterested.

Suddenly they saw the truck. A few yards to the right of it was the pillbox. Lloyd Owen decided that they could not keep calculating on an enemy's continued disinterestedness, and decided to wipe out the pillbox. Sergeant Hutchins went forward with some men and took it on. There was a brief moment when tommy-guns chattered. Silence. More gunfire. A few more rounds. Then silence. Sergeant Hutchins came back.

They heard the truck start—it wasn't badly hit, after all. So Lloyd Owen changed his mind about destroying it and went after the receding vehicle. A short distance away from the post the truck stopped and the men hurled themselves at the rear wheels, which had been punctured. For all the darkness they made a lightning change, while Lloyd Owen and the others stood out away from the vehicle, guns ready for any hostile action.

None came. Pantomime was rapidly becoming farce. They could wipe out an enemy outpost and nobody took any notice of the firing. And they could change wheels without bother, and finally drive away, victors of a second encounter with the enemy on his home ground.

But though they felt better because they had, after all, not lost a vehicle, Lloyd Owen was again having to worry over the swift-passing time. The night's plan demanded the taking of the enemy radar station by midnight, and because of the delays the L.R.D.G. captain was beginning to doubt that they could keep to the plan. He was still bothered about Haselden, sticking his head into the lion's mouth, and kept wondering what was happening near Mersa umm esc Sciausc.

Now they drove recklessly, trying to make up for lost time. They risked slit trenches, earthworks, boulders and strings

of barbed wire as they raced on towards the Axis road.
Here they turned right to join the main road into Tobruk.
They found themselves well within the enemy's midst now,
with tented camps all around and shadowy shapes showing
where enemy vehicles were dispersed to save them from the
nightly bombing raid on Tobruk.   They drove on, engines
roaring, with nothing to disguise them but the night itself.

At last they turned on to the main road.   They were
very watchful now, because they thought there would be an
enemy check post ahead and they were ready to fight their
way through it.   Their headlights picked out objects ahead
—something across the road.   The six vehicles slowed,
their crews very much alert.   In the light of their headlights
they saw a blockade of barrels and decrepit steam rollers
barring the way.   A formidable barrier.

The column stopped.   Lloyd Owen looked around.   He
could see defences and a ditch.   But there was no sound
from near by, just stillness.

Lloyd Owen got out and walked towards the barrier.
He called 'Rosalia!'   It was an Italian word—the enemy's
password—but it was no Italian voice that shouted it.
No one responded.

Thoroughly fed up now, Lloyd Owen looked at his watch.
It was one o'clock.   He looked at the solid barrier before
him and thought, 'There's no chance of getting inside
the perimeter now.'   Not with their trucks, which they
couldn't abandon, not in time to co-operate with John
Haselden and do their job of sabotage.

The most important thing was to get into touch with
Haselden.   If things were going all right with him, the
L.R.D.G. could still have a smack at the radar on their way
out before dawn, Lloyd Owen was thinking.   But if the
commandos had failed, all other action on the part of the
L.R.D.G. would be largely abortive.

So they stayed where they were, while a wireless operator
erected his aerial and then twiddled his dials.

Nothing came through.   Hour after hour the operator
tried to get Haselden, but every time failed.   Depressed,

worrying over the gallant commandos, Lloyd Owen kept walking about in the darkness, unable to keep still. Plans to release P.O.W.s and destroy radar were forgotten. The imperative thing was to know what was happening to Haselden so that new plans could be formulated so as to meet the situation.

There was an awful commotion going on in Tobruk, and they had a grandstand view of it. The gunfire and bombing seemed incessant, and the tracer and searchlights added to the entertainment.

But the majority of the L.R.D.G. just curled up and went to sleep, not bothered by the thought that they had come through the enemy lines and would have to get past them again before dawn. Let anyone watch the bombing raids; kip was the thing for them! And they kipped, leaving Lloyd Owen to do the worrying. . . .

Lloyd Owen saw headlights. Some vehicles were trundling down the road towards them. Something would have to be done about it, he thought, so he awoke the sleepers and prepared to receive visitors.

They had pulled their trucks off the road, and now Lloyd Owen went running up an embankment until he reached the tarmac. His men came behind him. Lloyd Owen walked down the middle of the road, tommy-gun ready for action. The headlights fell on him. The truck came straight at him, the driver probably recognizing him for an enemy.

So Lloyd Owen pulled the trigger, intending to shoot the truck to a standstill. Nothing happened. The bloody thing had stuck! He was in the way of the truck.

His men opened up and the night echoed to the roll of tommy-gun fire. The truck halted—very quickly. The L.R.D.G. came swarming out of the night and surrounded the enemy. They were Germans and very startled and apprehensive. One was an officer who could speak English.

Lloyd Owen questioned him. 'Where are you going?'

The German shrugged, 'Out of Tobruk,' he told them. There was nothing but chaos in the town, and he saw no sense in remaining there during the night. Lloyd Owen could learn nothing more from him, so he ordered his men to roll the enemy vehicles down the embankment. The men thought that Germans could lift heavy vehicles, too, and they were made to help tip their own trucks over the edge of the embankment.

That done, Lloyd Owen gave the signal for his men to pull out. He could not get in touch with Haselden, and he had a conviction now that things were anything but right down in Tobruk.

Searchlights were now combing out at sea, and there was heavy gunfire from what he knew must be the Navy. He was pretty sure by that that Operation Agreement had failed. Dawn was at hand and they had far to go.

They went back the way they had come, in the grey light of dawn passing enemy soldiers lighting fires for their morning cup of coffee, and travelling within yards of sentries sauntering with rifles slung over their shoulders. The L.R.D.G. had quite a race of it, in fact, getting through with little time to spare.

They stopped when they reached Sidi Rezegh airfield, and hurriedly set up their aerial and tried once again to contact Haselden. But still there was only silence, and after a while they went on to Hatiet Etla, there to wait in suspense for escaping commandos to show up.

XVIII

AT 0505 on Monday, September 14—D2 for Operation Agreement—one solitary searchlight suddenly abandoned aerial targets and flung itself out from the north shore. It wavered, touched *Sikh*, passed on, came back. Then it held the destroyer.

Sikh was picking up a dead motor-launch and two lighters. The set had brought them suddenly out of the darkness on to the stern of *Sikh* before anyone spotted them, and for a few frantic moments it seemed as if all the occupants would go under. The boats crashed against the *Sikh*, and some equipment went overboard, including a marine's rifle. Then someone cut a tow rope and the situation eased. Scrambling nets were thrown down and everybody hauled themselves up in the white light of the searchlight. Aboard the *Sikh* there was quiet activity around the guns.

As the marines came on deck an officer saw a man without his rifle. He gave the poor devil a lot of Army language, and then they were all sent below. Last man out of the boat was Able-Seaman Robinson, acting coxswain in a dumb lighter. It saved his life, being last.

A salvo came from some coast defence guns. As yet only *Sikh* was held by the searchlights, and *Zulu* turned and went out to sea for five minutes and then came in bow-on to the searchlights. Shells screamed through the night towards *Sikh*, beginning to turn away from shore after taking on the stranded marines. *Sikh* and *Zulu*'s gunners went into action and fired back, trying to hit the searchlights. South of their position it seemed as if every gun in Tobruk was now hurling tracer across the harbour towards other unseen targets close to Sciausc Bay. Then M.T.B.s were seen caught in searchlights and assailed by a fury of machine-gun and cannon fire.

More guns were firing all along the coast opposite *Sikh* and *Zulu*. Shells were coming closer. Then they began to hit. Mostly it was 88-mm. ack-ack stuff, and while it was disconcerting and did some damage, no one in the *Sikh* felt seriously perturbed. What was unpleasant was the fire from a coast defence battery about a mile west of the landing beach. This was bigger stuff, probably something like 5-inch guns.

Commander White could see the *Sikh* held now by two searchlights. He was perturbed to see the sister ship's behaviour. She was circling, losing speed. *Sikh* was already hit, mortally wounded at the start of the battle.

A big shell had landed in the forced lubrication system of the main engine gearing. The steering had also gone. Another shell had hit them for'ard and started a fire in the fo'c'sle It had also hit some ammunition stowed forward for ' A ' gun, and the blast came down into the messdecks and through a passage into which the returning marines were crowding.

Able-Seaman Robinson saw it all from the rear of the crowd. He saw the marines—those fine, healthy young commandos of a few moments before—go wilting in agony before the searing heat of the blast. Their bodies protected the *Sikh* seaman. The alleyway and mess decks were a shambles of burned and dying men. Worse, the fire for'ard had trapped many of the second flight of commandos, and it was impossible to get through to them.

Fire parties were being organized, and the wounded were being dragged out of the flames. But the ack-ack and coast defence batteries ashore were firing as fast as they could load at the crippled, almost motionless *Sikh*. She was a sitting target.

Her director-tower was next hit, and now her guns had to fire independently.

The Chief Engineer came to Captain Micklethwait and made his report. After which he said, in the emphatic

way of engineers, 'We must stop the engines or they'll
seize up without lubrication.' Which is an engineer's way
of seeing things.

Captain Micklethwait said, tersely, 'To hell with your
engines. I don't care a damn what happens to them, so
long as we get out of range of those guns.'

They were trying to steer a straight course, but the ship
would only turn slowly in circles. Then at last even that
stopped as the engines abruptly halted. *Sikh* lay helpless
and took the thrashing of her life.

At 0520 *Zulu* had been signalled that *Sikh* was badly hit.
At the same time Captain Micklethwait made a signal for
all Naval forces to retire. He knew that Operation Agreement had flopped. It was true that Colonel Haselden held
a bridgehead, and the land commando had succeeded
wonderfully in its task. But judging by the fireworks
display at the mouth of Tobruk harbour, nothing else had
succeeded. Clearly the M.T.B.s hadn't landed their forces,
and now never would in the face of such furious opposition.
And judging by the firing around Mersa Mreira the marines
had run into trouble, too.

It was a moment to write off losses, and Captain Micklethwait was a man who could do it. He gave the order to
retire—but there was no retiring for the old *Sikh*.

Commander White in *Zulu* now received a signal from
Sikh ordering him to take the helpless destroyer in tow.
This was at 0545. Since 0520 *Zulu* had been caught in
the searchlights and was being hit by shells, too. Both
ships had about this time begun to make a smoke screen,
but it was not very effective.

Commander White at once came racing in to take *Sikh*
in tow. It was coming light and suddenly they were hailed
from the water. They saw a motor-boat and three dumb
lighters drifting. Not only Colonel Unwin had had trouble
in keeping going, apparently. But *Sikh* was in greater need
of attention, and the tossing, awkward-looking craft had to
be left behind.

The first attempt to pass a line failed. *Sikh* was still

moving, very slowly but sufficient to upset calculations. *Zulu* manœuvred beautifully, bringing her stern round to meet *Sikh*'s bow. But the swell and the *Sikh*'s dying motions beat the manœuvre. *Zulu* just scraped the port bow and took away some stanchions. The line missed.

It was now almost daylight. *Zulu* circled again. More guns were ranging on them, hitting almost every time at targets no more than 2,000 yards out. *Sikh* was still firing all guns that could be brought to bear, smoke rising in a dense column from the bow where the fire raged. Another big-calibre shell hit them aft and started a second fire.

Then a shell exploded on deck near 'B' gun. When the smoke cleared, and the effects of the stunning violence had dissipated, they saw that only three men were left alive on the gun. Immediately a gun's crew formed from nowhere and got the gun into action again.

Zulu made another run. She came in, taking a lot of the fire on to herself, swung in from the port quarter, and a heaving line was thrown and made fast.

It broke.

Zulu circled for yet another run.

Sikh was swinging. Now only 'X' gun in the stern could be brought to bear. With one gun only she was talking back to a triumphant enemy that was hurling everything it had got against the destroyers.

But not just gunners were being heroic at that moment. The marines were fighting the fires now completely beyond anyone's control, and helping the crew wherever directed. Down in an engine-room *with a temperature of about* 180 *degrees*, the Chief Engineer, Lieutenant-Commander (E.) T. Lewis, was making attempts to get at the engines. The Gunner's Mate, H. W. Seymour, D.S.M., was down below, too, trying to fight his way through to rescue the marines trapped forward. Gillick, Rope, McManus—Electrical Artificer Taylor, Chief Yeoman Thatcher, P.O. Finn, Chief Petty Officer Moseling, D.S.M.—all were distinguishing themselves in those chaotic moments while *Zulu* came in for the third time to pass a tow-line.

Captain Micklethwait had a fine crew and some very brave and gallant officers. In the agony of those long hours of helplessness, he knew it. It might have helped if he had known that his men had those same feelings about their captain—that they took their inspiration from him; his bearing, his calmness, the way he gave his orders, kept them together and left them without personal thoughts that could embrace fear.

A shell exploded on the bridge, demolishing it and killing a rating. Captain Micklethwait had just gone for'ard.

Then *Zulu* came in. Commander White's handling of the craft was magnificent. Shells ranged her as she came across for the third time. Beautifully for a moment the ships were almost poised stern to bow. A line was cast—was caught. *Zulu* wasn't firing now, though 'X' gun continued on *Sikh*. Commander White had got every man on to the awkward wire hawser—every marine, including their O.C., Major Sankey. Hitting the enemy was of less importance than taking the *Sikh* in tow.

A rope was hauled across. The hawser was attached and began to go over. *Sikh* men grabbed it and made it fast. *Zulu* swung as her engines began to take the strain. *Sikh* started to move through the water. The batteries ashore were going frantic, cheated at the last moment of their target. . . .

A shell landed on the quarterdeck of *Zulu*. The hawser snapped. The tow had parted. Two men were killed on *Zulu* by that shell, and *Sikh* was helplessly adrift again.

It was a million to one chance, that happening—that a shell should land on a taut wire like that. But it had happened. And Captain Micklethwait knew it was the end. It was now broad daylight.

He refused to let *Zulu* take any more risks. He ordered her to stand away and not make another attempt to tow. Commander White at once signalled, 'Shall I come alongside and take off the ship's company?'

At 0636 hours Captain Micklethwait signalled back, 'Wait ten minutes.'

Commander White thought this might be to give *Sikh*
chance to hide herself in a smoke screen, and thus protect
Zulu during the transference, and he also came round on
Sikh making smoke.

Around seven o'clock *Zulu* was being repeatedly hit. The
big guns could get her range easily, and nothing Commander
White could do could silence the shore opposition. The
coast seemed alive with heavy guns pounding at the two
ships.

At 0708 Commander White received a signal. 'Leave
me and rejoin *Coventry*.'

It was a dreadful decision for Captain Micklethwait to
have to make, and yet his old friend, commander of the *Zulu*,
knew it was the correct one under the circumstances. Even
so, to *Sikh* it seemed as if *Zulu* was going to disobey and
come in yet again to try to take her in tow. Certainly for
a few minutes longer she laid down smoke to help her
stricken sister ship. Captain Micklethwait repeated his
order for *Zulu* to retire.

Then slowly, reluctantly, *Zulu* turned her bows seawards.
She made a signal to *Sikh*—'Good-bye. God bless you.'

Back came the *Sikh*'s reply: 'Thanks. Cheerio.' Captain
Micklethwait was an undemonstrative man.

When *Zulu* was six miles to seaward, she ran out of range
of the shore guns. The last she saw of *Sikh*, the destroyer
was on fire for'ard and aft, with tall columns of smoke
lifting to where enemy aircraft were beginning to circle.

But 'X' gun was still firing back at the shore batteries.

It was Black Monday for the marines and attached troops
also. It was a night of hell and agony for the first flight
in those Haifa boot-boxes. It had been bad enough getting
into the lifting, yawing, bucking cockleshells against the
side of the destroyers, but when the tow began it was
infinitely worse.

They had never been designed to cope with such a swell,
and a five-foot sea must have been running now. In the
blackness the men saw a faint sheen as the waves rolled in

towards them; the coffins rolled and seemed all the time about to go under. After a few minutes men began to be sick. Then nearly everyone was violently ill.

That was bad enough. But within minutes of leaving the destroyers the hopes of making a successful landing were rudely dispelled. The heavily-laden dumb lighters snubbed on their tow ropes with every fall of the swell. One after the other they parted until the darkness was filled with drifting, soldier-packed lighters and clumsy Haifa power-boats trying to find them and take them in tow again.

It was a fiasco. It went on for an hour for some, longer for others. All night long violently sick men had to seek over the side for frayed ends of tow ropes and then join them while their craft heeled before every sea and seemed on the verge of capsizing.

All too often, too, the parted tow ropes wrapped themselves round their propellors and there were long halts while swearing seamen went over the side to try to free them in the darkness. When eyebolts began to pull out of the lighters—those lighters designed with a view to economy—everyone felt it was the end.

Months of careful planning and preparation went by the board because of those wretched, unseaworthy boats; fine soldiers found themselves as helpless as children in the heaving night sea.

Then the searchlight came down over the waters, flitted over them, touched *Sikh*, came back over the waves as if to look for the smaller craft, then settled back on the destroyer. Guns began to fire from the shore. They could hear the whistle of shells over their heads, and instinctively ducked until they realized the target was *Sikh*.

Sikh. Too near the shore for a duel with coast batteries. Too near because of the dumb lighters which Captain Micklethwait had known could never make the long sea journey originally planned. Now *Sikh* was going to die because of false economy back in Haifa. 'Anything will do. They won't be needed after this one operation,' someone had said. 'Don't spend money on the things.' Perhaps those boats were going to cost the British Navy a few million pounds that night, as well as far too many lives.

Somehow, though, a few of the strings of craft made shore. Probably three landed with their lighters. It was the wrong shore. Everything had conspired to put them on the wrong beaches. Certainly there were no folbotists there, and at no time were signalling lights seen. True, there was one light, but that was inland and probably came from an Italian hospital camp; as they closed in on shore they began to see other flickering lights—perhaps a match lighting a sentry's cigarette, perhaps an oil lamp behind a swinging curtain to a soldier's bivvy. Too many lights in the end, but no Aldis lamps.

They hit the shore wherever the set threw them, but long before they landed they were under fire. Most of it was mortar fire, but plenty of tracer kept shooting out at them, and even bigger stuff opened up, the closer they came. Now they were saved only by the heaving seas, which made them erratic targets, low in the water and frequently lost to sight among the swell.

One string of lighters got ashore without loss of life. This was Major Jack Hedley's company of marines. The swell helped them, rolling them on to a shelving beach and throwing them out of reach of the waves. The men staggered ashore. It was getting light. When they looked their dumb lighters and Haifa power craft were being smashed by the waves. They would never return for a second flight.

But they were lucky. A few hundreds yards away another string of craft was being dashed to pieces on the rocks. In the half-light men were falling into the water, their equipment dragging them under, as the unwieldy craft hit submerged rocks. Men were being crushed to death between the boats and the rocks. Captain C. N. P. Powell, R.M., saw it happening and remembered how the men died without crying out; he wondered at it, even at that time and thought they were too highly trained to shout even in such moments. But one entire section was drowned within yards of their company officer, and there were others from the other boats, too.

Farther east still, Lieutenant W. J. Harris found his craft on the same submerged reef that had brought disaster to Peter Powell's party. All around, his men were dying, while the boats that had brought about their destruction shattered and broke up and sank.

Three parties of marines found themselves on shore. Three groups of officers held hasty conferences, none knowing that others had landed. They looked out to sea and in the growing light saw a crippled *Sikh* blazing fore and aft, and they knew there was no future that way for them. They knew, too, that with the enemy alerted, and time run out against them, Operation Agreement had sunk with the dumb lighters . . . they could forget it.

All three groups of officers made the same decision. They would fight their way through the Tobruk perimeter and try to escape into the desert.

The decision was almost instantaneous. Fire was beginning to bear on them and they started to move. Jack Hedley, a ranker before the war, now O.C. of B Company, led the way up a wide wadi that ran inland. They were on the outskirts of the town. The air seemed alive with planes taking off from El Gobi, and Tobruk itself appeared to be on fire.

Italians and Germans were beginning to appear in holes dug into the side of the wadi. It was quite clear that they had not been alerted, but very quickly they realized what was happening and got their guns and opened up on the marines.

From the beginning Hedley's company suffered losses. He had three officers and twenty-five men with him on landing, but within a few minutes several men were killed. One of the first to die was Lieutenant Hugh Dyall. Then Bill Palmbey stopped some M.G. fire and was hit in the leg. Hedley saw him go down. Palmbey just said: 'Well, I'm hit.' As if it surprised him. Hedley said: 'Hang on, Bill!' but kept going. There was no stopping for severely wounded under such fire.

They were vastly outnumbered, but the marines fought back magnificently. Nothing stopped them as they went up the wadi; they died, but far more of the enemy died, too. Sergeant Povall especially was covering himself with glory during the advance. Once Major Hedley was sure they were fighting in a minefield, but nothing happened, so they just went on.

It took them a long time to work their way against opposition up the wide, sun-baked wadi, and right at the last they found the stiffest resistance yet. Almost out of the wadi, Hedley began to climb the right-hand side in order to get a better view beyond. Suddenly he came under fire from a Breda across the wadi.

He saw coloured shells spitting towards him, and they exploded with devastating violence all too close to him. He got down under cover. Then some of his marines worked their way above their major and shot the Breda gunners. The advance continued.

Hedley had dropped his pistol in the sand. Now he was left with a grenade only. A big German sergeant appeared from a dug-out. Hedley said: 'See him off, Hunt!' Corporal Hunt saw him off. Next minute Hunt took a bullet clean through his shoulder but didn't realize it at the time.

Soon after half-past eight seventeen or eighteen marines found themselves out of the wadi. They had fought their way through the opposition, though they had lost three officers and six or seven men in the process.

Before them was open country. Hedley led his men across it at a fast pace. He wanted to clear the area before reinforcements came in, and his men needed no encouragement to keep up with him.

They found themselves in an inland wadi, as harshly forbidding as any around Tobruk. Hedley got his men under cover and told them to clean their weapons. When he looked out he saw Peter Powell coming into the wadi at a fine pace, leading about a dozen marines. Hedley at once went out to meet him.

Captain Powell's men had had to fight for their lives all the way inland. In the half-dawn they had found themselves being engaged by a machine-gun, but their Bren gunner soon put that out of action. Then, as they advanced, in the grey sky of half-dawn they saw the heads of enemy troops appearing. Everyone seemed to be moving in slow motion, but they were moving—moving and firing and clearing the enemy as they advanced.

The transport officer went down, shot high in the groin. Powell gave him a drink but had to leave him. They kept fighting their way inland, and suddenly they came out on more level ground where tents were pitched under palm trees.

The marines ran amok, trying to get through. They saw men moving among the tents and there was some firing at them, so they hurled grenades into the tents and sprayed any movement with tommy fire. They saw men tumbling out of beds with the force of the explosions, and there were cries of '*Mamma!*' and '*Aiuto!*'

Later it dawned on them what they were doing. Inadvertently they had fought their way into the hospital grounds. They were shooting and grenading sick and injured men in their hospital beds. But they weren't to know, at the time; there was nothing to tell them this was any different from any other enemy camp.

They fought their way through a shambles of collapsing tents that shrouded dead and dying, then found themselves climbing again. Moving across a wadi, they found themselves under fire from a Breda. They threw themselves into a trench. Another Breda got on to them, but perhaps it could not depress sufficiently and they found the exploding shells were hitting higher ground beyond.

They took a breather for a few seconds. The last minutes had been hectic. Powell found that both Bren guns were jammed, and there was no rifle that was not clogged with sand. He said, tersely: 'For Christ's sake, give them a burst with the tommy.'

But two hundred yards was too long a range.

They tried giving single shots with the Brens, but only one shot was fired before they jammed again. Powell broke open the bolt of a rifle with a stone and fired. The Italians lost some of their boldness and dodged down quickly.

While the enemy was on its face, Powell and his party clambered out of the trench and continued up the wadi. When he reached the head he realized they were within two miles of Tobruk. He began to head towards the main road, when suddenly Jack Hedley appeared.

Together the two officers made a hasty recce. They could see truckloads of troops being run into Tobruk. Out at sea two destroyers were still battling it out with the coast defences. Shells were falling not far away from the marines, but they weren't doing much harm to the desert.

The prospect dictated their next actions. They were within a few hundred yards of the main road into Tobruk and could quite easily see the constant string of traffic upon it. They knew they hadn't a hope of crossing the road unseen in daylight, so they decided to hide up for the day and try to make the desert after dark. They went back to their men to reorganize.

Powell sent Marine Linton down to a hut that overlooked the situation. Powell found he had ten men who could bear arms. Major Hedley had about the same number. The rest were more or less severely wounded. Surprisingly, they now found an R.A.F. pilot with them. No one was quite sure where he had come from, but it seemed he was one of the assorted bods taken aboard at Alexandria who had got ashore in the first flight. He was called Thomson, he said; his leg was very badly wounded but he wasn't complaining.

Major Hedley gave him and the other wounded morphia and got them to sleep.

Then Marine Linton came back with a report. He was a very calm man, not at all excited by their circumstances. He said that one of the destroyers was sinking, and the other was sailing off either on fire or making smoke.

Major Hedley went out at that. He stayed watching *Sikh* until the end; when she slipped under the water he went back to his men.

They were hiding in caves dug into the side of the wadi. There were hundreds of caves, and Hedley recognized them as old Australian defences from the time of the siege. The men were all well back, out of sight and sleeping away the effects of a very bad night. Hedley and Powell sat near the entrance of their dug-out and watched and waited.

They felt they were only a few hundred yards from freedom and safety, but the busy road was in between. But they were in a good hiding place, and so far there had been no sign of the enemy, except in the sky which seemed alive with roaring aircraft from El Gobi. If they could remain undetected until nightfall, they were confident they would make their escape. Once into the desert and they had a feeling the L.R.D.G. would show up.

For over an hour the M.T.B.s had been shot at. It had been an unrewarding night for them. Commander Blackburn had found himself with only six craft on arrival outside Tobruk harbour, and then after a couple of hours' probing he still had failed to find the lights at the entrance to Mersa Sciausc.

At some period during this time someone had closed in on Jermain's boat—he thought it was Commander Allan—to tell him that a signal had been picked up by one of the M.T.B.s announcing the success of Haselden's commando.

It had made things even more exasperating afterwards, to be fooling around, probably over a minefield, outside an enemy harbour. They knew that ashore the commando was depending on them, but they just could not see the lights. And yet they should have been seen.

Commander Blackburn went foraying in the dark around the entrance to the main Tobruk harbour. He felt he had to do something, having come so far into enemy territory, and he thought if he could find some enemy shipping and shoot it up they would feel better.

But there was no enemy shipping. Then Blackburn received a signal from Alexandria reporting that two M.T.B.s had found the landing-place and made a successful run in. That galvanized the prowling M.T.B.s and they swung east again to look for the lights. . . .

All at once there were too many lights. Suddenly every searchlight in the sky deserted the bombing planes and began to sweep the sea. The M.T.B.s for one startled moment were caught in the powerful beams. Then their craft roared into top speed and they went skidding away into the friendly distant blackness.

But they came back. They had to come back. They had invasion troops aboard. The Argylls and attached troops had been brought to effect a landing, and somehow they had to be got ashore.

Back came the boats, seeking a way past the barrier of lights covering the east point outside Tobruk harbour. Two M.T.B.s had found Sciausc Bay; the rest must try to find it, too.

Now, because of the blinding searchlights and the constant fire that erupted from the darkened coastline, it would be even more difficult to find the guiding Aldis lights. So the M.T.B.s began to run up to the boom defences across the harbour; finding them, they swung east and crawled slowly along the coast, hoping to dodge in under a searchlight beam.

But always the searchlights got them. Suddenly a powerful beam would swing on to them, then hold them like a spear impaling a victim. Only, the victim kept getting away.

But in the seconds while they were held, everything around Tobruk harbour came whizzing at them. The sky was a mass of flying tracer, and the air sang to the sound of unseen, spinning missiles. Strings of lights seemed to float in at them from every angle; the harbour itself was ablaze with lights, and from all around it ack-ack guns were now concentrating on the small boats.

Some M.T.B.s, seeing the hopelessness of the attempt to

run the gauntlet, had gone away again, seeking targets for their torpedoes. A few of them, more in bad temper than anything, let them go at the boom defences across the harbour—that harbour into which they should long ago have been sailing, if plans had gone right.

But nothing had gone right. Only Haselden's men ashore had done their work successfully, and even this knowledge was largely denied the world outside—including the M.T.B.s. At 0545 hours, in fact, Commander Blackburn had sent a signal to Force A that Sciausc Bay was in enemy hands. Yet it wasn't, not so early.

John Haselden still held a bridgehead in enemy territory.

XIX

THE game was up. Every man from Colonel Haselden down knew it. But they also knew that while the M.T.B.s were still trying to run the gauntlet outside Sciausc Bay, they had to stay where they were and hold the bridgehead. While there was still the remotest chance of pulling off Operation Agreement, they must stick to their posts. But no one felt very optimistic.

Now the men hugged the ground and moved from cover to cover. Patrols were out everywhere, seeking contact with the enemy. The fire upon the promontory was growing heavier every minute. Tracer was seeking targets on the headland. Already some men had been killed in the first attack. For the moment MacDonald, Barlow and their men were holding back a strong force of enemy troops west of the wadi.

A searchlight swung from the north shore, flickering over the headland. Then bigger guns began to shoot tracer across the bay towards their position. The place was becoming distinctly unhealthy.

Up on the west point John Poynton, guarding the vulnerable headland, watched a deadly game of hide-and-seek out at sea. Little ships like moths flitted into a moving pattern of searchlights that never for one moment left the entrance to Sciausc Bay unlighted, then seemed to fling away at top speed into the outer darkness of the Mediterranean. Each time an M.T.B. was caught, guns opened up all around the harbour, showering tracer towards it. Each time a young Naval commander took evasive action to escape the clinging searchlight beams and make for protective darkness farther off-shore.

That night John Poynton had proof that the Navy does not

give up easily. Right until dawn Poynton saw the M.T.B.s come creeping back, circling in towards the boom net across Tobruk harbour itself, as if to get their bearings, and then try to sneak into Sciausc Bay before the searchlights found them.

It seemed to the gunnery officer that there were seven M.T.B.s coming in in relays, being beaten off but returning time and again to try to make the landing.

But they had arrived too late. He kept thinking, 'If only they could have kept up with the first two. . . .'

Outside Sciausc Bay there was a position of stalemate. The coast guns might not be able to hit their nimble, elusive targets, but equally the M.T.B.s could not make the entrance to the cove without being blown out of the water.

A runner carried the news to John Haselden. Haselden had another problem on his mind. He said, '*What's happened to Colin?*' Nothing had been heard of Major Campbell and his party for close on five hours. He ordered David Sillito to take some men to look for the missing commandos. Sillito went off. He knew Campbell must have run into serious trouble. Long ago a simultaneous red-and-green Verey should have announced the capture of Mersa Biad, the next cove to Sciausc.

Followed by his men, he found himself hurrying through a minefield. It was a bad moment. Nothing happened, however, and they started to climb a rocky path beyond. Big S.S.M. Swinburn was behind the officer. In the darkness he felt Sillito halt abruptly. A Breda gun was pointing within feet at the Argyll officer's chest. An Italian soldier dimly seen was standing behind. He was staring at the kilted figure.

Sillito said, 'Yours!' and stepped smartly to one side. Swinburn, always the coolest man in action, did parade ground drill with his rifle. Lifted it. Sighted it. Fired.

They went on past the Breda. They searched the area, but failed to find any trace of their comrades.

Time was pressing. It must have been about five o'clock.

They were worried about Campbell and his party, and mystified by their non-appearance. But clearly, with an attack mounting on the cove, they could not stray too far east even in search of their comrades.

They began to retrace their steps through the lightening gloom down to the bay. One M.T.B. was still there, still hard aground. Its crew seemed to have vanished, perhaps departing with the other M.T.B.

A big figure resolved out of the shadows. Langton. He was breathing hard. The two officers hurriedly brought things up to date—Langton told of the last time he had seen Campbell. Both agreed that the London Scot must have struck tough resistance, something greater than had been encountered west of the cove.

Langton said he had seen what he took to be an M.T.B. signalling out at sea, but it had gone abruptly and nothing else had come close to the harbour. He said that it was hopeless, signalling any more. With the enemy alerted and bigger guns coming into action with the growing light, the M.T.B.s could never make land with their troops. He had left his torch shining from a crevice, all the same, and Scott was still signalling.

Then he told of his latest experience. Coming past the sangar he had run into two enemy soldiers. He had charged at them before they could move, and clubbed both with his revolver. But the diversion had caused him to lose his bearings slightly, and unexpectedly he had found himself in an enemy camp not very far back from the wadi —a place they had all missed in the previous search. He could hear men sleeping placidly, and he hadn't disturbed them but had circled the place and then come down on to the beach. The night was eventful enough even for Tom Langton, by the sound of it.

While Sillito and Langton were talking, they were conscious of the approach of dawn—the gaunt, tired faces of their men were becoming more and more revealed to them. They were now conscious, too, of very heavy firing. It seemed as though guns from all around the harbour were firing towards the headland, and there was heavy machine-gunning from inland, too. Added to this was the sound of their own two Vickers, brought in by the R.N.F., returning the fire above their heads.

Sillito went off hurriedly to report to Colonel Haselden. Tom Langton and Private Glynn set off once again to find the missing commando party. All they found was trouble. The enemy seemed to be waking up. Either that or they began to see posts missed in the dark by Campbell's party earlier. For half an hour the two blundered from one unpleasant situation to another, Langton using his revolver and Glynn his tommy-gun.

All at once it seemed to come light. What they saw along that desolate coast wasn't inspiring. They began to race back to the Italian house.

Weizmann and Wilenski, two of the Palestinians, were crouching along the wadi. The light was grey, the cold light that comes before the warming rays of dawning sunshine. All around they could see dark masses that were bleak, eroded rocky slopes. Firing kept coming from the shadowy grey distance, leaping little spurts of flame that told of enemy infantry crowding in.

But for the moment the firing was blind, intended to keep Haselden's scattered force under cover while a slow advance was made. What was more disconcerting were the shells that came screaming in across the waters of the harbour, from the big guns on the north side of the bay.

They kept landing on the promontory and in the wide wadi beyond. When the shells exploded there was a burst of flame and the rocks vibrated under the Palestinians as they hugged close to the ground to escape the flying splinters of stone and shell-case. Then dust and smoke drifted, dispersing slowly along the wadi, biting into their nostrils and leaving a sour taste in their dry mouths.

As they watched, one of the shells made a direct hit on a truck still at the point where they had debussed earlier. Flames licked up and then the truck really took fire and in no time there was nothing but a gaunt skeleton showing among the leaping yellow flames.

Then Berg came sliding along with three other men. They were searching for the Palestinians. They crouched together; Berg had orders from Captain Bray. He, Weizmann and Wilenski spoke in German, for it came most naturally to them.

Captain Bray said the game was up and attempts should be made to break past the enemy while there was still some darkness. The Palestinians were ordered to find themselves British Army clothing and destroy all German uniform, equipment and documents. The trucks, said Captain Bray, must be destroyed at the same time to deprive the enemy of two useful vehicles.

Berg went off with the three other men. Shells were bursting along the wadi. Weizmann and Wilenski slid off towards the blazing truck. Only one was left for them now to destroy. They started to look for the spare British uniforms that had been brought with them for this emergency. The light was bad but they searched diligently—and found no British K.D. Then they realized it must have been aboard the truck which was now a glowing wreck.

The Palestinians had no time to ponder on the problem. It was rapidly growing lighter. They had to move and move quickly before it was too late. If they were to be captured, it must not be in German guise.

They ran to the second truck. A lot of German documents had been left in the cab. These would betray them if they were caught, however they were dressed. They collected the papers, then threw petrol on the truck and set it on fire, running like mad for cover as soon as they did so.

Then they found a cave and went inside and stripped off every stitch of clothing. They piled it on top of the petrol-soaked German documents and, with fumbling hands, struck a match. Naked, they saw everything burn, stirring the ashes until nothing remained to incriminate them. Then they crawled out in search of uniforms.

But better to be captured naked than wearing anything German.

They started back across the hillside, following Berg and his companions. They found them—not Berg, but the three commandos. They were lying in grotesque attitudes where they had been caught by a shell-burst. Berg must have escaped the blast.

It was a repelling, nauseating thing they had to do, but there was no alternative. They stripped two of the dead commandos and put on their clothing. Then they went away, leaving two naked corpses to puzzle the advancing Germans.

In the Italian house Graham Taylor came out of his drugged sleep to realize that the drama was nearing an inevitable end. Dawn could not be too far away. The room was full of seriously wounded men. Captain Gibson had his hands full.

Graham Taylor felt curiously fit and strong, for all the plugs in his chest and back, and he sat up, a naturally active man rebelling at inactivity. He said, 'What's happening, John?'

Gibson's Canadian drawl said: 'We're just about finished, Graham. There's a damned army out there, bottling us in.'

'What about reinforcements?'

'Only two M.T.B.s ran the gauntlet. The rest are still worrying out there, but they won't get in. We've had it, chum.'

Graham Taylor got up shakily and began to walk about. Bullets were smacking into the walls of the building from three sides; Poynton with his men still held the rear. The wounded lieutenant was thinking, 'There won't be any destroyers to pick us up, after all.' No nice, pleasant getaway; no swift, comfortable (by desert commando standards) return to a civilization represented by Alexandria.

Haselden was directing the defence of the position, though he must have known it was hopeless. Swinburn had some of the men building a shallow, two-sandbag high wall around the base of the house. It was for a last stand.

Graham Taylor went outside, craving action though he could only move with difficulty.   He saw Captain Trollope lying almost under his feet.   The Signals officer had a rifle and was firing steadily at distant flashes beyond the wide wadi.   He seemed quite unperturbed, though performing a rôle unusual for him.   The two talked casually together in the dim light.

Captain Trollope said that a signal had been sent to H.Q., Alexandria, asking if Force A, the marine commando, had landed.   They were now awaiting the reply.   If the marines had succeeded in getting ashore, then Haselden and his men would have to keep on fighting here at Sciausc in order to embarrass the enemy and thus help Force A.

'And if the marines have not landed?'

Trollope reloaded.   'No one's got round to discussing that.   I'm in favour of getting aboard the wireless truck and just charging through them.'

Wounded though he was, Graham Taylor couldn't help thinking how out of character Trollope's proposition sounded. The Signals officer had never suggested dash and daring in his manner, yet now he was quite calmly, quite casually advocating bold measures.

Graham Taylor said: 'Good old Trolly!'   But he knew he couldn't go lurching about on any truck.   His chest wouldn't stand it.

John Poynton suddenly came haring up to the Italian house faster than he had ever sprinted for the Southport rugger club.   He came skipping neatly round the wireless truck, parked in some dead ground behind the house, and leapt for cover.

Haselden came forward.   The light was strengthening in the room.   The smack of bullets against the house walls was now quite a feature of the growing background noises. Distantly an aeroplane revved up its engines, preparatory to take off.   Perhaps the Stukas, they thought, said to be based on Gobi airfield.

Poynton wanted instructions.   It was plain to him that

Operation Agreement had been dead for a good hour now, and he was concerned about the coast defence guns he was guarding.

Haselden gave an order. 'Spike the guns, John. Then I think it's every man for himself.' A message was coming through in the corner. Captain Trollope came in quickly to take it. Haselden added: 'George Harrison and his sappers will return with you.'

They were saying good-bye, and both knew it. Haselden must have remembered the first time he had met the Royal Artillery lieutenant. John Poynton was also remembering it. Haselden had been in Ops Room, Cairo. He had turned at Poynton's entry and called him 'boy'. 'Get over there, boy.' And John Poynton had stood on one side while Haselden finished flagging—a map of Tobruk. From the first moment he saw Haselden, though, Poynton found himself attracted to the friendly senior officer; from that moment, like so many others in the commando, Poynton was an unchanging Haselden man.

Now Haselden's eyes twinkled as he said: 'You've earned your decoration, John.' He had remembered.

Poynton saw Trolly come forward with a signal. As Lieutenant Harrison handed him a pack of explosives to sling on his back, Poynton heard Haselden say: 'I'm sorry, chaps, but this is the end. It's every man for himself now, as I just said to John.'

They knew without being told what the signal contained. It said, 'Force A failed to land.' Time of origin was 0526 hours.

The knowledge had come too late. It was almost dawn. If they were to escape with their lives, they would have to break out into the desert, and light was no friend of hunted men. Again they thought of the huts with their awful heaps of mangled death, and none thought there would be any mercy for them.

Poynton went racing back with George Harrison and his sappers. The air was unpleasant with the sound of bullets chasing after them. In the distance to their right they saw a lone figure stumbling among the rocks. It was Pilot-Officer Aubrey Leonard Scott returning to base. He was hating it.

Poynton, Harrison and their ladened followers ran into the sandbagged enclosure of one of the gun-pits, without injury though they were fired on. The stolid Stanton and his three gunners were crouching at the entrance, guns ready for another attack. Poynton moved them out to safer cover and then the officers began to destroy the big guns, one after the other.

Across the bay, other crouching commandos saw the tiny figures of the officers working swiftly, dodging from gun pit to gun pit. Then they saw the guns shatter as the demolition charges destroyed them.

Now the watchers saw the tiny figures of Poynton, Harrison and their men break from cover and race along the high promontory towards the Italian house. It was broad daylight by now and a close-pressing enemy saw them, too. Fire began to sweep the headland. They saw a man stumble and fall, saw someone halt for a second, bend over him and then run on. Then another man went down. But the rest got through.

Poynton came charging into the cover of the Italian house, followed by the exhausted sappers and gunners. But Lieutenant Harrison wasn't with them. He had been killed in the race for safety; Poynton had seen that a bullet had gone through the R.E. officer's chest. Another sapper had died in the wild charge, too.

When they reached the house they saw that only a comparatively few men were there. There were no officers; Squadron Sergeant-Major Swinburn was directing a hopeless defence of the position.

Poyton told the S.S.M. what he had seen in the race to the house—armoured-cars moving in on the place and, he thought, tanks too.

Tanks. . . . And it seemed as if a whole brigade must now be closing in on the trapped men, while aircraft were coming up from the desert over their heads every few minutes.

When Poynton and Harrison went off to destroy the coast defence guns, there was a hurried conference in the Italian house. The concern of the officers was for the wounded.

Someone said: 'What about the M.T.B. in the bay? We can't all get away in it, but perhaps we could get some of the wounded to safety.'

Someone else said: 'The Navy couldn't get the thing off the rocks, so what chance have we? And how do we start the damned thing?'

Graham Taylor said: 'Well, it's no good staying here. Let's go down and try.' He wanted to move, to do something instead of just talking.

Herbert Bray appeared just then. It surprised some of them, because earlier he had disappeared on some mission, said to be in Tobruk town itself. Opinion was divided as to whether it would result in the capture of the German general or the release of the prisoners in the cages. Most thought he had gone prowling round the cages.

Bray looked quite unperturbed in spite of their grim situation. He and Lanark seemed quite sure of themselves, quite certain they would find a way out of this hole just as they had squeezed out of tight corners in the past.

One of the officers looked at Bray and thought: 'You won't rob the bank of Tobruk this time, Herbert!'

That was a bit of a joke among some of the officers. Bray had coolly stated one day that when they retired from Tobruk he would take with him the funds from the bank there. How would he break into the strongroom? Bray had got it all, as usual, nicely planned. He had heard of a safe-breaker aboard one of the destroyers; after the safe-breaker had opened the safe in the admiral's office, Bray was going to co-opt him into a private enterprise. Now there would be no chance.

David Sillito came pounding up the wadi then and hurled himself into the house. He made his report. Haselden was not happy. 'We can't wait any longer for Colin,' he told them. 'We'd better move.'

Graham Taylor said: 'I'll try to get down to the beach

with the walking wounded.' The men were brought in from the first-aid room. Some looked very bad, but they were still walking. As they slipped round the house to the shelter of the Afrika Korps marked Chevrolet, Graham Taylor heard Trollope say again : 'Let's put the rest of the wounded aboard the truck and smash our way through.'

Graham Taylor and the walking wounded passed the truck and began to descend the steep cliff path that led on to the sandy beach below. The last he saw of the fighting on top was a ring of grim-faced, begrimed commandos doing deadly work from behind the sandbagged defences. S.S.M. Swinburn was performing feats of heroism, seemingly oblivious of the storm of lead now assailing them from a wide crescent south of their position. And the blue shirt of Bill Barlow could be seen—Bill Barlow who hated to be called Hugh. He was revelling in the last-ditch fighting.

It was just about six. Taylor looked out over the sea. North of them, perhaps a mile or so out to sea, was a destroyer. It was on fire, a column of black smoke rising high into the glorious Mediterranean morning sky. One gun was firing steadily, replying to the bigger-gunned shore batteries that were smashing their shells unceasingly into the crippled, helpless ship. At sea to the east of them, a few M.T.B.s still circled, but were withdrawing as big guns east of Sciausc began to get their range in the growing light.

Taylor saw the grounded M.T.B. below, ensign fluttering. A beautiful ship. Then he saw a Carley float just passing through the exit to the bay, its occupants paddling for dear life round the corner. They were just out of sight when a plane came screaming out of the sky, the sea chopped by its strafing machine-guns in a long path that seemed to follow the unseen Carley float.

Planes were now taking off in constant procession from the nearby El Gobi airfield. They were roaring over the heads of the little group of defenders on the promontory, going out to sea, probably to bomb the destroyers and M.T.B.s, and then within minutes returning to land and load up with bombs again.

All at once a fighter with British markings came sweeping low over the defender's position. It cheered the men. If there was a British fighter here they felt less alone. Then they realized, as it circled slowly, that it was an enemy ruse to overlook their position. It was a captured British plane, gone before anyone could do anything about it.

Mike Roberts, who had been with Campbell's party, unexpectedly started to come up the path towards the slowly moving group of wounded. The tall transport officer had bad news. Campbell's party had encountered considerable resistance, Lieutenant Duffy had been killed in one engagement and Major Campbell had been shot in the thigh. They had suffered other casualties, too, among them Guardsman Hogan, who, responding tardily to a challenge, had been seriously wounded by one of his own commandos.

It was depressing news. One by one the commando was being wiped out. They halted to rest on the steep hillside. Some of the wounded could hardly move now. Overhead they heard the Chevrolet truck roar into life. Evidently Trollope was trying to make a dramatic break-out.

David Lanark, the Scots Guards officer, brought the truck to the side of the house. All the remaining wounded and a few men got aboard. But there wasn't much room for many, and few bothered to rise from behind the sandbag ring to get into the truck. Stoically they watched their comrades crouch down behind the steel sides, guns showing ready for the savage battle ahead. Lanark got out of the truck. He wasn't going with the party. Neither was Bray. Bray suddenly caught sight of the Palestinian, Steiner, in his German uniform, and said: 'For God's sake find some British clothing. Burn everything you've got on you.' He seemed undisturbed by the fact that he was still wearing German officer's uniform himself.

Captain Gibson climbed in with the wounded, and big Bill Barlow got behind the steering wheel. This was a job right up Barlow's street. He was grinning as he revved up the engine and engaged the gears.

They were about to start, the light getting quite strong now. Someone said: 'Where's Colonel Haselden?'

Then a man came running round the corner to the truck. He called out that there was a concentration of enemy across the wadi; the truck would be ambushed if it tried to drive through. Lanark, Bray and two of their S.I.G. followers, Berg and Steiner, immediately started a swift dash down the slope towards the threatened position. It was light, but still not quite light enough to make them obvious targets for the encircling enemy. They got through the bullet-swept open ground and dropped into cover. Private Watler caught up with them then.

And then they saw Haselden ahead. It was he who had first spotted the ambush. He must have run across immediately to tackle it single-handed. He was doing a good job of it, too. There were about ten Italians grouped behind cover to one side of the wadi, though there was fire coming at them from other, more distant points. The Italians had an automatic weapon with them, and the spray of bullets from it made them all dig down for cover.

But John Haselden did not go down for long. He kept jumping forward, his tommy-gun firing in short bursts. The Italians kept withdrawing. Haselden was shouting for support. Bray, Lanark and their men came round, hugging the cover and firing whenever they could. Back up the slope they could hear Barlow revving the truck engine.

Berg fell in the open, wounded, writhing with pain. Captain Bray leapt out, grabbed him and dragged him back under cover.

Haselden, still ahead, had driven the Italians well back from the rough track along the wadi. But the S.I.G. and Watler were running out of ammunition. Lanark sprinted back to get more rounds.

Barlow came roaring along in a bucking, bouncing truck, going at a speed never intended on such a broken surface. Haselden saw a threatening movement from the enemy. It looked a if they were going to attack the truck. He started a mad run right up to the Italians, shouting and firing the last rounds of his tommy-gun. The Italians were yielding, breaking up and running before him. Barlow and the truck got safely through and went careering noisily out of sight. The wounded had been saved—for the moment, anyway . . .

Haselden was down, within ten yards of the enemy. He was lying on his face, still and silent. Fire was sweeping across the area from several positions now. Steiner, his gun empty, crouching behind uncertain cover, kept shouting above the din: 'Colonel Haselden! Colonel Haselden!' He was watching the commando leader for a sign of life. There was none.

Then the long-legged Lieutenant MacDonald seemed to come from nowhere. Steiner saw him race up to Haselden. Mac's hands were outstretched to pick up his colonel. He was beginning to bend over him.

A stick bomb skipped through the air and landed on Haselden's back. It exploded. Mac was hurled back by the force of it. He staggered under cover. He was stunned, his face blackened, yet miraculously he was otherwise unhurt. Watler grabbed him and dragged the officer back to the pathway that led down to the beach.

Steiner looked again at his colonel. John Haselden, gallant gentleman, was dead. Steiner found Berg and helped him down to the beach.

David Lanark was on the M.T.B. He had brought the boat's twin Brownings into action and was spraying the wadi where Haselden was lying. When he came racing down he had found Tom Langton and Glynn on the boat. They had been searching for food and water. David Sillito came down. He had suddenly decided to abandon his kilt, because Scots were especially marked men to an enemy who hated the 'ladies from hell'. So, reluctantly, he had hidden the Argyll kilt in a cave and found himself some shorts.

MacDonald, Steiner, Watler and the wounded Berg came down into the bay. There was a hurried consultation. Enemy fire was sweeping across the beach. Their position, crouched around the M.T.B., would soon become untenable.

Above their heads, out of sight round the wadi, the bulk of their now much-depleted commando were making the fight of their lives in a last stand around the Italian house. Somewhere on the winding pathway Graham Taylor and his walking wounded must have been resting. On the west point, little running figures would be George Harrison and his sappers performing a last-minute act of sabotage to frustrate a soon-to-be-victorious enemy. On a ridge south of them, two Vickers roared furiously; Sergeant Miller, M.M., and his gallant R.N.F. were giving 'em hell.

Mortars had been brought up. The bombs were beginning to fall around the Italian house. The end was not far off. The beleaguered little force under Sergeant-Major Swinburn could not escape now; they could only fight on. Down in the wadi there seemed no chance of returning to Swinburn and his party. Their thoughts turned to escape.

They had the means right there beside them—that fine, fast, undamaged M.T.B.—but nothing they could do would move it. Langton had been over it thoroughly but couldn't even start the engines; as he explained: 'I just don't know which buttons to push.'

So they had to abandon it regretfully. They all piled into a float alongside the M.T.B. and began to paddle out through the entrance to the bay. Machine-gun fire suddenly came sweeping at them, the sea boiling all around them just as they came round the east point. There was the deafening noise of a diving aircraft all too close to them. They shouted and paddled furiously, pulling into the next bay east—Mersa Biad. The sea was too hostile for them. They got on land and split up. Little parties went scurrying for cover, dodging away like hunted rats among the rocks already hot from the morning sun. All the way marksmen took aim at them and fired; only their fine commando training saved their lives during that desperate, last attempt to break into the open desert.

David Sillito and Bill MacDonald clambered eastwards hoping to be able to signal to some M.T.B. off coast, though none could be seen now. Langton and Glynn, officer and private, co-drivers of a truck all the way from Cairo, sparring partners and good comrades, said good-bye to each other; Langton was going to walk back to Alamein if necessary, Glynn didn't like walking and was somehow going to join his comrades in the last stand under Sergeant-Major Swinburn. Lanark went loping off with Weizmann and Watler. Bray suddenly appeared and took the other men with him. Bray, of course, had his own plans.

He was damned if he was going to do any walking. He thought he could return in style. He knew where there was an Italian camp on the main road. Bray's plan was to walk into the camp, grab a truck with plenty of food and water and drive off into the desert. He felt pretty sure he could do it, too. With his S.I.G. men, Berg and Wilenski, and several other commandos from Major Campbell's party, Herbert Bray blithely struck inland for the main road. The commandos had bobbed up from nowhere; there was still that pantomime quality about the whole affair, with people appearing and disappearing and then running into each other again.

The commando was disintegrating. The end for most of them was inevitable, but no man yet thought of tame surrender.

Barlow had come to grief in his truck. No one quite knew what had happened, but the one thing certain was that he had failed to break through a heavily reinforced enemy.

On a ridge east of the Italian house, Sergeant Miller's R.N.F. were doing stirring work with their machine-guns. Their fire, more than anything else, was holding the enemy in check across the wadi. But ammunition was running low. Each gun had already used eight belts.

Bill Barlow came scrambling up to them, under fire all the way. He wanted covering fire to get his men and the wounded up from a pocket along the wadi. Miller knew his job. It meant re-siting his guns so that they could cover the crest of the hill opposite. He gave his orders.

Two little teams worked frantically to move guns and

ammunition to the new positions. Miller's team—Lance-Corporal Ridley, Fusiliers Harbottle, Shields and Mac-Donald. Corporal Wilson's—Lance-Corporal Watt, and the identical twins, Fusiliers A. & G. Leslie. They knew that everything around them was failure, but they had ammunition and they were still following orders.

Their Vickers machine-guns roared and a disconcerted enemy dragged itself away from the ridge opposite. Barlow and his men came up in a rush, dragging the wounded with them. Barlow seemed quite cheerful. He gathered his little force together, including the R.N.F., and told them the situation was hopeless. Their only chance was to try to work their way either into the desert to meet a wandering patrol of L.R.D.G., or they could make for Mersa Shegga, nine miles along the coast north of Bardia, where on the night of D6/D7 an M.T.B. was supposed to pick up stragglers.

He ordered the R.N.F. to destroy the guns and attach themselves to his party. As Miller had used the last round of ammunition, he immediately spiked his gun and they all set off. They kept running into other little parties. Sergeant Evans who had been with Major Campbell, joined them. Then Tom Langton. Then they ran into Lanark, Weizmann and Watler. It would have been sociable, but big parties were against their chances of survival. Plane after plane was scouring the area, looking for them.

Lanark organized things. He divided food and water, split them into parties again, then set them off at ten minute intervals on different bearings.

Pilot-Officer Scott had sent his runner in to H.Q. long ago. Now he was wishing he had started off earlier. The hills all around seemed to be crackling with small-arms and machine-gun fire. Bullets were ricocheting with terrifying screams from rocks all around him. He kept clambering on, dodging from cover to cover, waiting for opportune moments to continue his dash. It was far too light for his comfort. He didn't quite know where he was going, or why he was moving at all; all Scotty knew was a hunger for companionship. He had spent a lonely night, and if it was his time to die he would like it in friendly company.

It took him a long time. While he was still painfully scrambling up the high, rocky hillside, a German E-boat came quickly through the cove entrance and opened up with its guns, raking the wadi walls all around. It did some damage—to some German troops closing on the east side of the wadi. Elsewhere the commando watched with satisfaction while the E-boat shot up their own men. Then the E-boat went out of the bay just as quickly as it had entered.

Scott saw friends in a pocket between him and the Italian house. He started to run. Bullets made him skip. He went even faster and came hurtling into cover undamaged. Someone turned on his stomach and said: 'I don't know how the devil you got across there, because they were all firing at you.' Scotty didn't know, either. But he didn't mind. He was among friends. He felt better, took out his .45 and looked round for an enemy.

Lieutenants Roberts and Murphy were there with some of their men. Mike Roberts had brought in the wounded Campbell, who was in a bad way. From somewhere, too, Roberts had 'accrued' about sixteen Italian prisoners. The Italians were lying on their faces in a shallow depression on the north side of the house, in deadly danger from the shells and bullets of their comrades and allies.

In the daylight the defenders in and around the Italian house could see a massing of the enemy among the rocks before them. Heavy fire was pouring in on them; always there was constant movement as enemy infantry slipped from cover to cover . . . always nearer.

Poynton and Swinburn lay side-by-side, watching. They saw a big attack develop: all at once Germans and Italians were trying to storm their position under cover of heavy machine-gun fire. They fought back furiously, and after what seemed a long time, the attack faded, and the fire slackened momentarily. But Poynton thought, 'This can't last. Another time. . . .'

There was no thought of surrender among the defenders yet. They still had ammunition, and there was a lot of fight in the men. But Poynton did not like their position. They were being steadily outflanked and were under enfilading fire from machine-guns.

He told Swinburn that he would take a party of men to a ridge behind them; Swinburn would give them covering fire, and when Poynton was in position, Swinburn could follow with the rest of the men.

Poynton called to the men who had been on the guns with him. Some ack-ack gunners also got up to follow him. All at once Poynton made a dash towards the ridge, the men following. Swinburn and his men began a heavy fire to cover their withdrawal. Bullets were flying back, when a curious thing happened.

Poynton found himself stumbling over the prone bodies of the terrified Italian prisoners. Suddenly they all jumped to their feet and began to run with Poynton and his men; Italians and British ran side by side, comrades in fear for the moment. The fire along the wadi slackened as the Italian attackers saw the danger to their comrades.

Poynton saw his opportunity. He ran behind the group now, shouting and kicking them the way he wanted them to go. Those watching him thought he looked like a sheep dog snapping on the heels of . . . sheep.

But his manœuvre succeeded. He drove the Italian prisoners up the hill and over the ridge, his men running safely among them. Not a man was hurt, but in the last seconds Poynton was nearly killed as heavy machine-gun and Breda light cannon fire sprayed the ridge top as he dived for cover.

Poynton and his men got down behind the ridge. The Italian prisoners kept on running and weren't seen again. Intensive fire was directed against the ridge now. Peering down at Swinburn, crouching alongside the Italian house, Poynton saw the big sergeant-major wave his arms in a signal which plainly meant he could not follow. A second party could never get across that open ground and remain alive.

Poynton and his followers were on their own. Worse, mortars were already rangeing the ridge. Poynton said: 'We've got to keep moving.' He could just see the M.T.B. down below on the sandy beach, pennant flying. To reach it, though, they would have to cross another ridge. Poynton led the dash. This time there was no protection because of stampeding Italians, and a furious fire came after them. In the short dash for the second ridge Bombardier Bedward and Gunner Riley, both ack-ack men, were killed, and some of the others wounded.

Over the ridge, they began to slide down the slope towards the M.T.B. It seemed too good to be true. Here was an apparently unhurt boat that could take them back to Alexandria. Then Poynton saw khaki-clad forms. More of the commando. They swerved and ran towards them. . . . The commando was wearing German helmets. There were a lot of them. Poynton came to a halt. They were almost out of ammunition. This *was* the end.

He raised his hands in surrender. His tired men did the same.

Everybody kept running down towards the M.T.B. It was tantalizing, too obviously the only way of escape, and yet out of the question because it was hard aground.

Graham Taylor was on the beach with Captain Gibson and some of the wounded. They must have got there just ahead of John Poynton and his gunners.

The wounded lieutenant had tried to shift the M.T.B. but it never moved a fraction. So they all went and took shelter in a cave because the air was alive with noisy, speeding bullets. Someone else slipped into the cave and joined them; he told them he had seen Barlow's blue shirt in the far distance. Barlow was being hunted by a force of Italians among the rocks. And Barlow had been walking around sniping casually with his rifle as if he were still on that duck shoot.

About this time Graham Taylor realized that in some caves near by them were about fifty Italians. They must have been there all the night.   They continued to stay where they were.   If the war had come to Tobruk, here were fifty Italians who knew their own business and were keeping right out of it.   *Viva Mussolini!*

Out at sea Stukas were diving at unseen targets and bombing and strafing them.   They would be the M.T.B.s, the weary, depressed men thought.   The day was golden with sunshine, the sun hot upon the bleached and arid land. It was a fine day for men facing the consequences of failure.

Then they saw another E-boat nosing cautiously into the bay.   Graham Taylor promptly drew his revolver, wounded though he was, and said, 'I suppose we'll have to fight it out here.'

Captain Gibson made a rude Canadian remark, grabbed the gun and hurled it into the sea.   The time for fighting was over.   Gibson went out into the open, holding his red-cross bag prominently before him.

German sailors came inshore.   They looked very young, very fresh and clean.   They were smiling.   It didn't seem possible.   They were gentle with the wounded, taking them aboard and giving them hot drink and food.   All except Graham Taylor who was now a stretcher case and couldn't stride the short gap between a rocky ledge and the E-boat.

But weak though he was, Graham Taylor was still very much conscious.   He heard remarks from the young German sailors.   They were delighted with the performance of the commando.   Haselden's men had smartened up their Italian allies, they said.   Nothing pleased Germans more than to see their Axis partners humbled a bit.   And the commando had humbled them more than a bit; by the sound of it, an atmosphere of hysteria was rampant over the entire Tobruk Italian garrison, where they awaited a major offensive from an Allied task force which surely must be supporting the handful of commandos at Sciausc Bay.

XX

THE *Sikh* was dead under the feet of her captain. Now all that could be done was to bury her, so that no enemy could take her and use her against the people who had made and loved her.

It was Captain Micklethwait who had to put her below the lifting swell there a mile or so off the Tobruk coast. He gave an order: 'Prepare to abandon ship.' 'X' gun was still firing at shore targets. They were probably doing no damage, but the men wanted to go on firing, and Captain Micklethwait let them use up the last of the ammunition because it helped the morale of his crew.

The *Zulu* was racing away over the horizon. When it was beyond range the shore gunners concentrated on the stationary *Sikh*. Now the one helpless destroyer took all the fire from the coast batteries. Shells exploded almost continuously against the sides of the battered vessel. Every minute added to the devastation aboard what had been a beautiful ship.

The men went about their work of abandoning ship as if they were ignoring the heavy fire upon them. More shells completely demolished the bridge. Aft, the fire swelled up as a succession of shells got in and added to the holocaust. Then 'X' gun ran out of ammunition.

Even then *Sikh* did not take her battering passively. Any man who felt so inclined walked up to an Oerlikon and belted off a pan of ammunition if it made him feel better. It probably didn't hurt the enemy but it did them good to feel they could still hit back.

Lieutenant Nickolls got rid of ninety rounds that way at an unseen aircraft. Captain Micklethwait had ordered: 'Nick, get some fuel oil and scrub that damned Italian sign

off our deck.'   Nick was searching for the oil when he heard
the order to abandon ship.   He had promptly gone to an
Oerlikon and blazed away, and then he felt a little better.

Everything floatable was going over the side.   They
were without their usual boats for such an emergency,
because the assault craft had displaced them on the deck.
And they had something like seventy marines in addition
to her large crew aboard, though many were trapped forward
and probably dead by now.   There would be no boats for the
survivors: even the motor-boat with its dumb lighters had
drifted away in the effort to escape from the first shore salvoes.

Carley floats went into the water.   On a shell-swept deck
men hastily lashed rafts together and lowered them into the
heaving sea.   Scrambling nets went in; their corks would
hold a man up.   Odd spars, wooden debris from below—
anything that would support a man—went over the side.
For the *Sikh* had a crew of over three hundred men, and with
the surviving marines this meant that a lot of floatable
debris was required.

Paymaster-Lieutenant Elliott found himself curiously
involved in a scene below.   Elliott had prepared the ship's
documents for sinking.   They were in a canvas bag eye-
letted to let out the air when thrown overboard.   But the
drill for ' *Documents, ship's, sinking of* ' called for weights in
the bag, and the paymaster-lieutenant could only think of
ballast (iron bars) for the purpose.

So he went down to the engine-room and spoke to the
chief stoker.   He needed ballast urgently, he explained.
The chief listened not without sympathy, but finally shook
his head.   There was his point of view to consider, he explained.   The ballast was his responsibility and if people
went chucking it over the side he might 'get a bottle'.

He was very firm about it, too, but in the end Elliott got
his ballast and the bag went bubbling down to the ocean
bottom.

About eight o'clock everything was ready.   The crew
saw Captain Micklethwait, very grim, give the order,
'Abandon ship.'

It was a bad moment. The men knew what was in store for them. If they survived the next hours, it would mean at the best that they would become prisoners-of-war. That was no prospect for men who valued their freedom. But there was more to it than just that, hearing the order to desert *Sikh* in her moment of death—they were seamen, with a love of their ship, and no man serving the sea can abandon his ship without hating the moment of parting. It seemed something like a betrayal.

Yet instinctively those men of the *Sikh* knew that their depression, their suffering, was nothing compared with that of their captain. For a ship is her captain, and Captain Micklethwait felt himself part of the ship he had been so proud to command. The grimness of his face told his men what he was going through at this moment, and they knew what dreadful task was ahead of him . . . he had to sink his ship with his own hands when they were safely over the side.

A big battle-grimed stoker suddenly marched forward, seemingly oblivious of the shellfire. A startled Micklethwait saw a man whose hair had been singed off, an apparition of a seaman, holding out his hand. He heard the man say 'Good-bye, sir. Sorry this happened.'

And then the man was over the side, and another man had taken his place. They were queuing up to say good-bye and good luck to their captain; momentarily they weren't bothered about their safety, about the scream of shells that lashed into the ship. No man would go before he had paid his respects to a commander who would not long be with them.

To Captain Micklethwait it must have been a moment of mingled pride and agony. It was a tribute beyond any decorations that a grateful country might bestow. The grimness left his face; men saw him smile, and they felt the warmth of this man who had been a fighter and whose fighting days were over.

Then they were all over the side, swimming in the water and clinging to the drifting spars—all except their captain. The wounded were being lowered on to the rafts, so far as they were able to hold them. It was a ghastly business.

Men—mostly the marines—were shockingly burned as well as wounded. Some of the men had every square inch of skin burnt from their tormented bodies. Now the salt waves swept up, splashing them on their rafts. The air was awful with the sound of men screaming, of men crying to be pushed off the rafts and held under the water so as to end it all quickly. And other men, injured themselves, held them back and wouldn't grant them a wish that would have been a mercy.

The ship's medical officer, Lieutenant-Surgeon Barry O'Neill, was going round in a float, seeking out the worst injured and trying to help them. They could see him, someone holding down a moaning, struggling, flame-licked creature while the M.O. injected morphine that was not always of any use.

A great mass of wreckage drifted over a wide area, hundreds of men clinging to it, the sun pouring down on them. For the unhurt it was pleasant enough, but for the wounded, especially the marines with their awful burns, the sun, wind and salt were hell. The screaming never seemed to end, torturing the swimming, helpless men who had to listen to it.

All eyes watched the *Sikh*. They were remembering the battles they had fought and won—nineteen Malta convoys that had been escorted with three other destroyers; their part in the sinking of two 8-inch Italian cruisers in the Pantellaria Straits. And they had taken part in the Battle of Sirte against the Italian Fleet, apart from anti-submarine actions and successes. They had all gone through hell aboard their gallant ship, and they felt she deserved a better fate than to be sunk by her own captain.

Captain Micklethwait had kept back one officer, Lieutenant-Commander D. S. Smith, and two men to fire the demolition charges. Another officer, Lieutenant John David, did not go over the side with the others but stayed close to his captain. David, the ship's navigating officer, had been Captain Micklethwait's right-hand man throughout the planning of Operation Agreement, and in fact had selected the rehearsal area for the marine landing force off the coast of Cyprus. Micklethwait guessed that the young officer was concerned about the way his captain might take the loss of his ship, and was staying behind to keep an eye on Captain Micklethwait.

They went below when the charges were blown and saw the water pouring into the engine and boiler rooms. Sending the demolition party over the side, Captain Micklethwait and Lieutenant David made a final tour of the blazing, sinking ship to make sure that no one alive was left aboard.

When they came up on deck again they saw their men, hundreds of them, silently clinging to their floats, drifting away from the ship. Shells were screaming over the heads of the men in the water with unabated fury. Just occasionally one fell short and men died in the midst of the wreckage in the sea.

Suddenly a shell exploded on the deck close to the officers. Micklethwait saw Lieutenant David fall, hit by a splinter in his head. It added to Micklethwait's grief of the moment, because he was fond of the younger man.

He picked him up, thinking he might still be alive. The deck was too hot for comfort, and Captain Micklethwait knew it was time he went after his men. He slung David on his shoulder, then walked over the side of the ship into the sea. When he surfaced in the water he realized that poor David was dead.

Micklethwait began to swim over to where his men were drifting. Unexpectedly a man came swimming up. He said, 'Here you are, sir.' Micklethwait was astonished to see him proferring a lighted cigarette. He didn't smoke, but he accepted it because he knew that the man wanted him to take his gift.

He was still wondering how a man could light a cigarette while up to his neck in water, when another grinning seaman swam up holding a bottle . It was rum. The man said, 'Have a swig, sir.'

Micklethwait had a swig. He knew he was going to need it. Perhaps that was why the men were trying to help him. He turned on his side. *Sikh* was going under.

But she seemed reluctant to go. It must have taken

half an hour before finally she slid under the blue Mediterranean waves that had borne her much of her grand life.

The men watched her go in silence. It was a bad moment.
Captain Micklethwait's eyes never left her. He was not
far from weeping, the mourning of a brave man at the passing
of a gallant creature. He kept thinking, 'She was a living
thing.' A living thing mortally stricken, then dying silently
—now going . . . gone. Not just so many tons of steel and
wood, but something which had lived and been loved by
all who had served in her. They all felt it, hanging on to
their spars and rafts.

Then the sea was empty where before the big, graceful
destroyer had been.

The men relaxed. The shelling ended. They had lost
their ship. They were going into the bag. Their captain's
promising career was virtually ended.

For what?

So that opposite them Major Hedley and a few marines could
make a gesture—could fight because they had been trained to
fight and had come all this way to fight. So they were fighting.

And south of the harbour, in an area littered with corpses,
the last of Haselden's commando could hold on, sure of
death when their ammunition ran out. Men who had
succeeded, only to find that all other plans had gone awry
and they were now . . . expendable.

A hero came down from the sky, strafing the men in the
water. Some thought it was a bomb attack, but it was
cannon fire exploding among them. A man died and others
were injured. 'Brave bloody bastard!' shouted the impotent
men, and watched it circle to come diving in again at them.

But this time the hero conserved his ammunition. Perhaps
even he saw no medals in strafing helpless seamen.

For about two hours they drifted, the worst injured finally,
mercifully dying and sliding into the water and then slowly
sinking away. Two hours of agony for the horribly burned
marines, with the sun blazing upon their raw flesh and the
salt water washing it and adding to the torment.

Two hours . . . Haselden's men had had orders not to let

any craft slip out of the harbour. Whenever the enemy small-boats tried, Haselden's men opened fire on them, holding them back for quite a long while.

Captain Micklethwait was still in command, still with fight in him. One of the motor-boats with its dumb lighters had appeared from along the coast. Micklethwait ordered all the rafts and wreckage to be brought together and made into a tow behind the motor-boat. It began to assemble, a fantastic train of floats, spars and nets. Micklethwait's idea was to use the current to drift them past the entrance to Tobruk harbour, calculating that they would beach somewhere east along the coast. Then parties would make escape bids into the desert.

It was a forlorn hope, more of a gesture than anything, doomed to failure for most if not all, as the captain well knew. But while there was a chance of escape or of embarrassing the enemy, they had to take it.

They took it. The motor-boat could do about four knots with three dumb lighters in tow; with its train of wreckage its speed was reduced to about one knot. At this speed they tried to escape from the enemy.

It was during the time that the tow was being assembled that Captain Micklethwait witnessed what seemed to him to be courage of a very high order. When the motor-boat and dumb lighters came up, Micklethwait swam alongside them. A wounded man was being supported in a scrambling net. Micklethwait said, 'I want you to make room for this wounded man.'

He was looking at a marine in a lighter. The marine at once stepped into the water. Most of his companions did likewise. Many of the marines were non-swimmers, but they almost scrambled to get into the water to make room for the wounded. Micklethwait looked at the marines, few of them regulars, and thought them superb.

About ten-thirty, with the firing ashore weakening every minute, a steel landing-barge, flying the Italian flag, came up the coast to meet them. They knew that their desert plans were ended then.

It was a sturdy craft, unaffected by the swell that had made
their plywood boats virtually helpless. The marines looked
at it and said, 'If we'd had boats like that, we'd all have got
ashore.' And if they'd got ashore, the marines would have
done their job. Operation Agreement might have been
pulled off.

Then they heard an order from Captain Micklethwait,
being passed from mouth to mouth along the line of clinging
men. 'We're going to take this barge when we get aboard.
Be ready!'

The *Sikh*'s crew braced itself. They weren't going into
the bag without a last struggle, they determined. They
saw guns pointing at them as the barge came slowly up.
Italian faces looked at them in triumph, it seemed to many
of the crew. Then they began to take survivors aboard.
Wounded men first. Then the rest of the marines and ship's
crew. And then Captain Micklethwait.

An Italian leaned over to help the *Sikh*'s captain. They
saw him throw aside the helping hand. There was contempt
in the gesture. Then Captain Micklethwait pulled himself
easily into the barge.

With dawn the raids began on the hovering small craft
still remaining outside Tobruk harbour. Fine seamanship
had kept them intact during the bombardment from the shore
guns, but these raids by Stukas were something far worse.

As the bombers sought out their targets and came screaming in to the attack, the M.T.B. crews, assisted by Argylls,
R.N.F., and attached troops, fired everything they had at the
planes. Their firepower was tremendous for such small craft;
the fury of it must have been intimidating to the Stuka pilots.

But all the same, some ships suffered. One blew up with
a roar that rolled miles into the hills west of them. Another
was hit. Then an M.L. caught fire. To the watching
Argylls it seemed as if the three bigger M.L.s had gone
inshore to draw the fire. One *had* drawn it, and there was
no helping it with its deck cargo of petrol roaring into a
mighty column of flame.

Captain MacFie had grown hourly more concerned because no landing had been effected. He had even argued
about the matter with his skipper, but at sea the young
naval lieutenant was in command and it was MacFie who
had to take orders. Those orders were, 'You will stay where
you are until I can land you in the right place.'

So a fuming, fed-up, battle-trained platoon saw the dark
hours pass into daylight. It became all too apparent that
Operation Agreement was ended. Then they were brought
on deck to man the guns and fight back the Stuka raiders,
who were to attack them all that day and until late in the
afternoon.

All that day . . . with losses all the way.

Lieutenant Ernest Raymond of the R.N.F. was not taking
the situation easily either. But he had heard that two
M.T.B.s were ashore, and without proof he was fairly certain
they were his boys who had landed. Now he wanted to
land and go to their assistance. He could hear firing ashore
and saw obvious signs of battle; and his men were in it and
he felt he ought to go to them and share in the fight.

He demanded of his skipper that all craft in the area be
brought together; he thought if he landed at another place,
perhaps on the north shore, they might yet hurt the enemy
and bring a relief upon the hard-pressed Force B, including
his R.N.F. section.

The M.T.B. skipper gave a flat, 'No!' and went on
dodging bombs with a nonchalance that impressed the
Army lieutenant. And 'No' it had to be.

There were only four M.T.B.s and two M.L.s in the harbour entrance now. The rest must have slipped off along
the coast in the early morning hours after receiving a signal
missed by the other craft. They were like lost people, not
wanting to leave without orders, yet not seeming to receive
any on their wireless receivers.

Then it was that Lieutenant Charles Coles saw the non-
combatant. It was during a vicious raid, with every
available man firing or bringing ammunition to the gunners.

The non-combatant was hauling ammunition as if his life depended on it. When the raid was over and the men were relaxing preparatory to taking on another Stuka, Coles called down to the R.A.M.C. sergeant, 'I thought you were a non-combatant?'

The man turned. There was a self-conscious grin on his face. He said, awkwardly, 'Let's forget about that, shall we?'

Then they saw the *Zulu* detach herself from her sister ship and come circling towards them. At times some of the M.T.B.s had been within five hundred yards of the battle between the destroyers and the shore guns. *Zulu* was gathering speed, but to the men on the smaller craft it was obvious she had had a mauling, and it seemed as though she was listing.

The M.T.B.s and M.L.s closed in on the bigger ship, like children seeking instructions from a parent. It came through a loud hailer. 'Clear off. Make your way independently to Alex.'

Commander Blackburn called back, 'May we go to the assistance of *Sikh*?'

Back came the reply, 'No, I regret she must be left.'

The destroyer and the smaller craft parted, the M.T.B.s and M.L.s taking the shortest route possible down the coast because of their scant fuel supplies, the *Zulu* seeking safety out to sea.

It was not a moment that anyone liked. It meant running away from a trapped force who had expected to be evacuated by sea. But nothing could be done to help them. no craft could get inshore now. Haselden's commando was on its own.

And all the while enemy aircraft were lifting from El Gobi airfield. They were roaring over the heads of Sergeant-Major Swinburn and his last-ditch defenders, diving in on the scattering naval craft, bombing and strafing and then turning back to bomb up and take off again.

That day there were hundreds of sorties against the forces taking part in Operation Agreement.

XXI

THE end was near for the last of Haselden's commando. They knew it, but they went on fighting because there seemed nothing else for them to do but fight.

There was fighting across the harbour, too, somewhere back of the town among the rugged rocks so like those around the Italian house. The commandos guessed they would be marines, hopelessly trapped like themselves, and by the diminution of fire they knew the end was near for them, too.

The harbour was placid and blue, and the sea beyond serene and friendly after its malignant uncertainty of the past days. The sun poured down upon them: it was too warm, too hot upon prone, sprawling men who had gone too long without sleep and had fought hard and been without food and water beyond the normal limits of fighting men.

But while they had ammunition they went on fighting. They wanted to live and they were sure the Italians would kill them when they saw those shelters. So they went on killing more Italians, and occasionally a German, too, as if that would help them when the end came.

Overhead the bombers took off and roared out to sea, then after an interval came back and then took off again. The harrying of the Naval forces was going on. The commandos had no time to wonder what was happening over the blue horizon. Closing in on them was an Italian battalion, the Battalione San Marco, along with Germans. The high ground around them seemed alive with troops, crawling forward towards their position. Eastwards the enemy had closed the gap through which some of the commando had escaped earlier. Now there was no escape. . . .

Earlier, not much after dawn, they had all thought themselves saved. They had seen a line of troops advancing from the direction of Tobruk town, and they had thought them to be marines, working their way round to their rescue.

But when the commandos stood up, cheering, a Spandau opened up on them. They weren't marines—they were Germans.

The commandos put up a heavy fire and held back the enemy while some of their number made a double-strength sangar between some metal sheds. The sergeant-major and eighteen men went into the sangar, and eight men took over the sandbagged porch of the Italian house.

It was curious . . . interesting . . . the mood of the last commandos. They were certain they were going to die. That was why they fought on, to live another few minutes, to see the world for a little while longer.

But curiously their nearness to death was in no way terrifying to them. On the contrary it seemed to exhilarate them, to affect them almost as alcohol might have done. They were lying across each other to fire, because there was little space behind the sandbags, and they were talking and joking, lighting cigarettes for each other, and all the time taking deadly toll of the advancing Italians and Germans.

Some enemy infantry were behind cover no more than fifty yards away, and the commandos never missed when they saw a target at that range.

Someone said: 'This is better than Butlin's.' Billy might have been surprised at the comment.

They had tried to clear away the too-near enemy by throwing grenades, but they had failed to clear a ridge and the bombs had started to roll back upon the defenders before exploding. It was getting their own back with vengeance, and the commandos soon stopped throwing grenades.

Big Swinburn took a hand then. It was all heroically foolish and reckless, but that was their mood at the moment. The hell with risk, in a minute they were going to die!

Lying on his side behind the sandbags, a commando held wide the neck of a sandbag. Swinburn swiftly drew pins from two Mills bombs and dropped them in the sack. Almost in the same second the big sergeant-major leapt to his feet, whirling the sandbag round his head and then flinging it over the ridge. The extra leverage gave him the distance and the bombs went off where the thrower had planned.

Swinburn should never have lived to do that twice, and was a bold man to try it again. He did it several times, though, and each time by a miracle escaped injury. The sacks of grenades cleared the ridge, bucked up the commandos by doing so, and no doubt did Swinburn a bit of good, too.

It was senseless resistance. There could only be one end to it. But they didn't fancy the end and were determined to hold the fort while ever they had ammunition.

One trouble was that the commando's arms were mostly unsuitable. Few had brought rifles with them, and more than anything rifles were needed now. Tommy-guns hadn't the range and were forever sticking. Armourer Sergeant Alford mended two tommies when the fire was at its hottest, but they were of little value for sniping warfare.

Then a machine gun opened up on the sangar from a good position and their shallow sandbag defence fairly danced under the heavy lead. Swinburn decided to put an end to that, too.

He knelt, Bren gun against his hip, and fired back. The enemy machine-gun fire ceased and Swinburn dropped quickly down into cover. He should have been dead again, but for some reason wasn't.

He was an inspiration to his men, the calmest, seemingly most unruffled man among them. If he was worried about the next moments, he failed to show it, and because of his courage his men reacted similarly. While he fought, so would they. But it couldn't go on much longer. They had only survived so long against such opposition by a miracle as it was.

All at once they realized that the Italian house behind them had been captured and with it the eight defenders on the sandbagged porch. Now they were on their own in the sangar between the tin huts.

A German potato masher (mortar) had them nicely ranged, too. A bomb crashed through the roof of the shed to the rear of the sangar. Another blew up right in front of their sandbags. If either had landed within the sandbag ring it would have been all over for the lot of them.

Apparently other Germans had moved into a good position, for suddenly a German stick bomb came floating through the air and landed against Private MacKay's left foot.

He was wedged on his side, unable to move, so he shut his eyes and wondered what it would be like to be without a foot. It exploded. That was all there was to it. An explosion and no one was hurt and MacKay still had his foot. But everyone was past marvelling at the freak results from explosives.

Their fire had almost ended. Most had no more than two or three rounds left for their guns. Swinburn realized that all faces were turning to look at him—sweat-stained, bearded faces, faces drained of hope or any other human emotion.

They heard him say, abruptly, 'All right, lads, that's enough. Pack it in now.'

So they packed it in, just lying besides their useless weapons and wondering what was going to happen in the next minutes when the Italians got hold of them. By now the enemy must have found their dead.

They saw Swinburn roll over, very deliberate at the last. He was removing a shirt that was a long way from whiteness but was the best he could manage under the circumstances. Then he stood erect, and held the shirt above his head.

To some of the men this was in itself an act of heroism. Swinburn had stood up while a hail of bullets poured across towards their sandbag ring, and that took guts. And again he was unharmed.

The firing stopped. To the men lying at the feet of their sergeant-major there was something uncanny about the silence after the constant, unceasing barrage of sound that

had lasted for over fourteen hours now. They heard the
final echoes go ringing among the barren rocks, and then,
bone weary, they climbed to their feet beside Swinburn,
their hands slowly lifting above their shoulders. This was
the end. No getaway on a destroyer, after all. Not that
they blamed the Navy. The Navy would have got through
if there had been half a chance.

They saw movements among the rocks. Then a uniform
showed. Then all at once a lot of soldiers were standing
cautiously erect behind their cover. When it was seen that
this was no ruse but a surrender, the enemy came surging
across towards the British soldiers. Hundreds of armed
men seemed to be racing to reach them first—the area before
them was suddenly solid with eager, blood-thirsting enemy
troops, and they were shouting and screaming abuse as they
came running near. The commandos instinctively bunched
closer, yet they knew it was hopeless. To some of them it
was like the end of an international match, with a horde of
excited spectators racing to engulf the players. Only these
had no friendly intentions.

But it was a German who reached them first, another
big officer. He looked very clean and soldierly, a handsome
man, and he had been wounded. And his first words
knocked the wind out of the taut, expectant commandos.
Astonished, they heard in perfect English, ' It was a very good
fight. Congratulations.'

But the Italians, who were in a majority, had other
thoughts. They came surging in, their faces suffused with
rage, demanding fearful vengeance. One smashed a blow
across Swinburn's mouth. He just took it, continuing to
stand there, blood trickling from his lips, his face impassive.

The Italians were milling round the helpless commandos,
shouting for the lives of the men who had slain their comrades
in the night. They wanted their heads, and they brandished
their guns and knives and fought among themselves to get
at the motionless, helpless commandos. For a moment it
seemed as if some blood-crazy Italians were through and
coming in to kill the little group.

And then some Germans seemed to appear from nowhere and got in the way. The Afrika Korps men shouted at the Italians and shoved them back every time they tried to break through. Again it was like an out-of-hand mob at a big match, with a thin line of police trying to hold them back. Only, these police were also enemies, the Germans.

The brawl went on for quite an hour. It was a crazy scene, with the Italians wanting to kill the commandos and the Germans determined to save their lives. Sometimes the Italians seemed to be gaining the ascendancy, other times the Germans were browbeating their allies.

By this time the commandos couldn't care less what happened. Suddenly they all felt too whacked to bother even about death. They craved to be given a drink, and after that to be allowed to rest. They sat on the nearest rocks and rested their hands on their heads and waited for the numerically superior Italians to win.

But the Italians didn't win. The Germans weren't giving any victories to a nation which failed to make their own in battle. They kept shouting and shoving back and in time the Italians grew tired of it and gave in. But it was a treacherous capitulation; their sullen faces and angry eyes told a nearness to over-boiling again. The Germans grouped around the commandos and watched closely the allies they detested.

It must have been near to twelve o'clock when Swinburn's men realized that it was a reprieve. Then another German told them quite pleasantly that they would have to go into Tobruk, but there was no transport for them and it meant walking all the way.

A weird procession set off—the commandos in the midst of the protective Germans, with hundreds of Italians milling around, shouting abuse and threats but doing nothing more than that. It was a long walk, with their wounded to be helped along, a wearying walk of defeat. It seemed an eternity before they reached Tobruk, and then their sufferings began again.

They were treated like wild beasts and herded into a

special prison compound that was stiff with heavily armed guards. And they were starved—hardly given any food at all—for the next few weeks in an effort to weaken them and break down the commando initiative which might cause them to break out and run amok through a Tobruk that had had enough of commandos.

They were going into years of hardship, captivity and sometimes death, those remnants of gallant Haselden's commando.

Captain Micklethwait, earlier, had met a resolute Italian: 'The only resolute Italian I ever ran into in my life,' he said afterwards.

When all the *Sikh* men and marines were aboard the landing barge, they began to attempt to capture it. All at once men began to sidle towards the bows, where a solitary Italian stood above them behind a machine-gun. Suddenly they had a feeling this mightn't be too difficult. The Italians were a slack shower and might easily be fooled. . . .

An Italian behind a machine-gun crouched, sighting along the barrel, and shouted to them. They didn't understand a word, but they knew what he was saying. One step more and the whole lot would have it.

That was the one resolute Italian of Captain Micklethwait's life.

XXII

ANOTHER brave ship was about to die. The tragedy of Operation Agreement seemed without end.

At 0630 hours on Monday, *Coventry* and the eight 'Hunt' destroyers had returned almost to Alexandria, this according to plan and with a view to confusing enemy radar along the coast which might otherwise have been interested in *Sikh* and *Zulu*.

Abreast of El Daba, so close to Alamein, they had seen the port under bombardment from the sea, and guessed it was the cruiser *Dido*, with the destroyers *Jervis*, *Javelin*, *Paladin*, *Pakenham* and *Kelvin* creating yet another diversion from Operation Agreement.

It had been an anxious night for *Coventry's* commander, Captain Dendy. There had been the delay in receiving the success signal from Haselden's force—it had finally reached the cruiser at 0210 hours, far later than had been expected. Captain Dendy had been about to despatch a signal bringing Operation K into force, the plan for the abandonment of Operation Agreement, when finally the codeword 'Nigger' came in from Alexandria.

Captain Dendy had expected attack from E-boats, brought out by the bombardment of Daba, but rather to everyone's surprise Monday night was without hostile incident.

Then suddenly the long silence was broken by Force A. It was not a happy signal that came to Captain Dendy. At 0526 came a signal from *Sikh* that she had been hit. Then at 0630 hours a signal came from Captain Mickleth-wait ordering the withdrawal of all Naval forces from the Tobruk area.

Simultaneously, Captain Dendy received a signal from the

C.-in-C., Admiral Sir Henry Harwood, ordering Force D to turn and steer for a position approximating to the point of release of *Sikh* and *Zulu* the previous night.

This set a problem for Captain Dendy. Most of Force D had travelled from Port Said to Tobruk and back at speed; now they were expected to sail almost as great a distance again, and all without refuelling. Captain Dendy's worry was that if they met trouble on the way, involving side excursions for the squadron, some of the 'Hunts' might run out of fuel.

Coventry, he knew, would be all right, but first he had to know the fuel position on the destroyers. The reports, when they began to come in, indicated a critical position. They had nothing in hand for special actions. Before all the reports reached the Force D commander, however, two signals came in quick succession from *Zulu*.

The first said that she had parted from *Sikh*; the second that she had been hit.

The latter signal seemed to indicate to Captain Dendy that *Zulu* was badly hit and could only travel at slow speed. His appreciation of this, in regard to fuel reports from the destroyers, still coming in, was that most of the 'Hunts' would not have enough fuel to meet *Zulu* and escort her back at slow speed.

It was a perplexing situation. Then came another signal from *Zulu* saying she was now making thirty knots. It appeared at the time to help in making a decision. Captain Dendy sent *Aldenham* and *Belvoir* in for fuel, an unfortunate choice, as he was to realize later. With six destroyers around him, he crowded on all speed to try to meet *Zulu* before she got into further trouble. It wasn't a healthy place for a limping ship, off the enemy coast and near to so many hostile airfields, and besides a submarine had been reported in the area. True, the plot was a day or so old, but the submarine might still be lurking in the track of *Zulu*.

Force D had had a fighter cover of Beaufighters since daybreak. They were scouting well out from the force, without contacting any enemy. At 0915 Captain Dendy received orders from Alexandria to stand further away from the coast; his fighter escort must have reported his position as being too near to a German airfield, probably at El Daba.

Captain Dendy turned in a northerly direction with the intention of sailing on this course for two hours before turning west to intercept *Zulu*. Then, reaching *Zulu*, they would race at *Coventry's* maximum speed (about twenty-two knots) for Alexandria.

Five minutes before the two hours were up, Captain Dendy received a further signal from *Zulu*. This gave a corrected position, as a result of which *Coventry* at once turned west to meet her. By their calculations they would intercept the 'Tribal' destroyer at approximately 0130.

There had been threats of air raids from about seven that morning. Practically all the time there had been signals on the radar of various unidentified aircraft in the distance. However, none had come in to a range closer than about eighty miles, so that no one was greatly worried in Force D. Nevertheless it was quite obvious that Force D was being shadowed.

At 0830 Captain Dendy decided to try to drive away the presumed hostile aircraft because *Zulu* was getting close. He broke R/T silence and tried to put his fighter escort on to them. There was considerable trouble in establishing radio communication with the Beaufighters, however—altogether it had been a miserable time for signals—and it was two hours before effective sea-air co-operation began. Then one Beaufighter was sent above the clouds to maintain patrol and if possible identify the aircraft. Nothing happened. Cloud was down to about four thousand feet and there was no contact and no combat.

At eleven-fifteen *Coventry* with six 'Hunts' was steering on two-seven-o' degrees, expecting to see *Zulu* in about two hours. The radar screen was showing two or three groups of unidentified aircraft following a long way off, and a few minutes earlier Captain Dendy had again put his fighters on to them—without any result.

Suddenly Captain Dendy got a shout from his fighter

directing officer that a large number of aircraft were coming in to attack from the stern. For a moment a Beaufighter had broken cloud, and seen the threat and passed on a swift warning. The *Coventry's* radar, one of the oldest in the Service, was good at long range, but not so good close to. For some reason it had not reported the developing attack. Later there was talk that the enemy bombers came in making an I.F.F. signal (a signal which indicated that the planes were British or Allied) but there was never confirmation of this.

At 1124 hours there was no undue cause for alarm aboard the *Coventry*. At 1126 she was a broken, useless ship.

Fifteen Ju 87s suddenly broke cloud, diving at devastating speed upon the fast-steaming ship below. Captain Dendy turned as fifteen dive-bombers released their missiles at the ship. His after guns leapt into action without orders and the rest immediately they could bear on the target. All around him six ' Hunts ' tried desperately to throw up a protective barrage to cover the bigger craft.

At least four bombs hit the ship. She was a shambles, stricken and helpless all in one second.

One bomb hit her bows for'ard of No. 1 gun and blew them off, reducing her at this point to the waterline and starting a fire. The second and third bombs exploded on the fo'c'sle deck under the bridge, demolishing everything underneath the compass platform, and penetrating the deck below, started a smaller fire. Captain Dendy was on the compass platform with other personnel; miraculously no one was hit or hurt, though the ship rocked to the violence of the blows, and bomb splinters slashed through the air all around them. But everything underneath was destroyed, and everybody immediately below was killed.

The fourth bomb hit abaft the after funnel. This exploded in a boiler-room, wrecking it, at the same time destroying the radar transmitting room. The scenes below when rescue teams ran to help the injured were horrifying. Most were past help. In one fraction of time sixty-three officers and men had gone out of existence on the *Coventry*.

Machine-gun and cannon fire strafing the deck had added to the chaos following the bomb attack.

All ship's communications had been severed. The ship was losing speed. The dazed crew began to recover and put preliminary damage control into operation. Captain Dendy ordered the *Dulverton's* captain, senior officer of the 'Hunts,' to radio a report of the incident to Alexandria. Then he went to inspect the damage more closely.

They were on fire for'ard. Captain Dendy ordered the flooding of a four-inch magazine to prevent a further explosion, but they could not get to a pom-pom magazine because of the fires raging around it. The bridge structure was on fire, and the boiler room out of action. The bow was damaged in a manner which precluding towing bow first. He found they could move slowly astern on one engine only. They would have to go over to hand steering, and they were without radar or wireless.

All along the deck, amid the torn wreckage, were dead and dying men. Casualties were high, but Captain Dendy realized that they would have been far higher if the standing order—that all personnel must wear anti-flash clothing while at action stations—had not been obeyed on the *Coventry*.

No man appeared to be suffering from burns or flash wounds. The men had groused about wearing the clothing, unpleasant in the heat of battle, but now they were going to reap the benefit, even though most failed to realize it. The *Sikh* marines, in their K.D. shorts and thin shirts, in their agony in the salt water, could have told them of the blessing of protective clothing. . . .

The fires were spreading; the heat as the flames fanned across the deck was appalling. Foamite had been rushed up, but the pressure was too low and anyway it could not be positioned to attack the worst fires.

Captain Dendy had to make a decision. He thought that the *Coventry* could be saved, could be towed into Alexandria. But at what cost?

He knew that such a slow-moving target would attract

enemy bombers from all along the coast, and while daylight lasted, *Coventry* and her escorts would be the object of sustained and ferocious attacks. In attempting to save the old girl some of the 'Hunts' would for certain be severely damaged, if not sunk, and many men would assuredly die. Besides, there was a crippled *Zulu* needing all the protection that active 'Hunts' could give her.

Captain Dendy gave an order. It was: 'Abandon ship!' Then he went resolutely about the task of sinking her: another captain hating what he had to do, yet having to go through with it.

It was a bridge decision, drastic and taken alone. He ordered *Dulverton* to signal his intention to his C.-in-C. At almost exactly the same moment the C.-in-C. signalled to Captain Dendy to sink the crippled *Coventry*. The signals must have crossed . . . it must have been some consolation to Captain Dendy to know that his decision had been the correct one in the eyes of his C.-in-C.

It was from this moment that Captain Dendy found fate completely against him. It was bad enough to lose his ship, to have to destroy it himself—and their Lordships of the Admiralty are singularly cool towards ships' commanders losing their craft under any circumstances. But now Captain Dendy began to feel that there was a conspiracy to prevent the destruction of the old cruiser.

Some time back, upon his orders, the scuttling charges had been removed and unprimed. Now they could not be got at, and consequently Captain Dendy was unable to scuttle his ship.

The charges had been removed because of an experience a few months earlier. This was when *Coventry* was one of the escort with a convoy to Malta. The battleship, *Centurion*, was in that convoy, and in the event it never got through.

The *Centurion* discovered that whenever she received a near miss—and she received an awful lot on that convoy—the scuttling charges promptly blew. When she returned to Alexandria she was drawing something like forty feet of water.

That was something which Captain Dendy did not wish to occur in *Coventry*, which invariably drew enemy aircraft on to her whenever she left port. The ship already drew enough water—more than most cruisers—and her captain did not see why she should go down because of a near miss. So the scuttling charges were unprimed and removed. Now the action, again correct at the time, was against Captain Dendy.

A second bitter blow was to follow.

Captain Dendy ordered *Dulverton* to sink *Coventry* with her torpedoes. But Lieutenant-Commander R. T. Wilson of *Dulverton* gave him astonishing information.

The six 'Hunts' circling protectively round *Coventry* were no longer fitted with torpedoes. The only 'Hunts' in Force D with torpedoes had been the two sent back to Alexandria for refuelling—the *Aldenham* and *Belvoir*!

Captain Dendy must have felt the fates were truly against him now. His ship was lost to him, but he had no means of sinking her. Yet somehow she must be sunk; she could not be left drifting off an enemy coast.

For a long time now men had been going over the side of the ship and were swimming in the water, those for whom there was no place in the boats or on what rafts had survived the swift bombing attack. They had been clinging to wreckage thrown overboard, taking things quite cheerfully, watching the prowling 'Hunts' and wondering when they would come in to pick them up. The swift little destroyers seemed a long time in closing in on the stricken ship, but the 'Hunts' were still watching their radar screens for further enemy attacks; they didn't want to be caught, stationary targets alongside the dead hulk of the *Coventry*.

But at last two destroyers detached themselves and came circling in, slowing as they neared the *Coventry*. Scrambling nets were lowered and the survivors picked up. Then *Beaufort* moved in on the cruiser, and the badly wounded were brought across.

Captain Dendy took the ship's documents and books, then made a last search of the ship for anyone living. And then, last to leave the old *Coventry*, Captain Dendy got on to the *Beaufort* by climbing out over the anchor.

The 'Hunts' then tried to sink the cruiser. She was a wreck and fiercely on fire, but she would not sink. They came close and hurled four-inch shells at the vessel, but she had a three-inch armour belt to penetrate and the damage done seemed inconsiderable.

It was infuriating, but finally they found a solution.

The *Zulu* would have to torpedo her as she came hurrying by.

The little ships were being chased all the way back to Alexandria. From dawn until almost sunset, throughout the long day one or another of the depleted fleet was being strafed or bombed. Dozens of Stukas were out, searching the ocean for sign of the boats, streaking at about forty knots towards safety. When they were found, down would come the dive-bombers, letting rip with their guns and coming in close to drop their bombs at the twisting, dodging targets.

The Argylls and R.N.F. welcomed it. They felt they had been cheated; they had trained for action but then had been brought away in a manner they felt to have been somewhat ignominious. So now they took it out of the dive-bombers. They crouched on the decks of the bucking, rearing, fast-speeding M.T.B.s and as the Stukas came in they fired everything they had at them—rifles, tommy-guns, Brens, Vickers, Lewis guns, even revolvers struck back at the enemy.

It must have been intimidating. The fire power of the M.T.B.s was formidable. The fury of their defence plainly turned away some of the attacks. And there were claims by M.T.B. personnel of crippling hits that spelled the end of some 'dirty great Stukas'.

Raymond's R.N.F. were certain they had made a kill and were jubilant about it. One Stuka came diving in almost on to them before letting go with its bombs. Their concentrated fire was seen to tear holes in the wings, and when it pulled away it seemed unable to climb, and finally they saw a tall column of smoke over the horizon just where it had disappeared. Claiming a share of the credit in the kill was a non-combatant, as noisily delighted as the rest.

But not all boats got away with it as that one did. The M.T.B.s and M.L.s suffered all the way down that hostile coastline. Sometimes Messerschmitts joined in the attack, but it was the Stukas that were mostly to be feared. Some of the Stukas carried sirens, and when they came screaming down in what seemed a never-ending dive the crescendo of sound was appalling and demoralizing.

The bombers got three more M.T.B.s and two of the three M.L.s during the long run down the African coast. All the others were more or less severely damaged.

The M.L.s, slower than the M.T.B.s and larger targets, soon drew the attention of the enemy. M.L.353, commanded by Lieutenant E. J. Michelson, R.N.Z.N.V.R., found herself continually assailed by cannon-firing Macchi 202s. They came in with well-synchronized attacks, and inevitably M.L.353 was soon disabled in spite of a whole-hearted resistance.

M.L.349, commanded by the senior officer, Lieutenant-Commander Ball, came back and embarked the crew of the striken ship and demolition charges put her to the bottom.

Then the attacks concentrated on M.L.352 (Lieutenant G. R. Worledge). The Macchis kept coming in. The hard-pressed guns' crews fought back for hours, while Worledge took evasive action to avoid the savage attacks. But time after time the M.L. was hit. After a while the petrol tanks were so damaged by shell fire that petrol poured out into the bilges, and the crew were fighting in a floating shell of highly inflammable petrol.

A Macchi came in, defying the furious fire that rose up at her, her cannons lashing a line through the sea that ended with the 352. There was a tremendous explosion that ripped forty feet out of the port side, and the ship became a mass of flames. Even so, gunners on the for'ard gun continued to fire at aircraft which dived again and again to pour shells and bullets into the dying M.L.; the gunners went into the water when all their ammunition was exhausted.

When the swimmers were four or five hundred yards from the M.L. she went up. Hours later the survivors were picked up by the Italian destroyer, *Castore*.

The elusive M.T.B.s fought a longer battle. One of their problems, though, was the spare petrol stacked in cans on their decks. It was reserve fuel, necessary to get them back to Alexandria, but it was a constant source of danger every time bullets or cannon-shells came strafing the nimbly dodging targets. In the end it brought disaster to one craft and near disaster to another.

M.T.B. No. 266 (Lieutenant Richard Smith, R.N.V.R.) witnessed two instances of ships being fired from the air. Running fast down the coast shortly after daylight, he saw a fighter attack develop against two other scurrying M.T.B.s.

The first to go up in flames was Lieutenant Alec Foster's. He and his first-lieutenant, Nick Illett, achieved the seemingly impossible and put the flames out.

There were Argylls aboard that boat. They were firing up at a diving plane. A spray of cannon shells came lashing down on them. One hit their deck cargo of reserve fuel, and instantly the decks were awash with blazing petrol.

Some of the Argylls thought that one of the M.T.B. crew immediately slipped into an asbestos suit and went below, switching on their main engines. Whatever happened, the M.T.B. suddenly went tearing away, the skipper somehow contriving to ship a wave which washed the blazing petrol into the sea. Dazed Argylls, clinging for dear life to the ship, found themselves standing on a deck burned almost completely through. But it got them back to Alexandria.

In the same swift, savage attack, Smith saw another M.T.B. go up in flames. Jan Quarrie's M.T.B. caught a packet and became an inferno in seconds. Argylls were aboard this ship, too. They went leaping into the water to escape from the roaring flames; a few launched a collapsible craft and scrambled into it.

266 came round to pick them up. The assault craft came paddling frantically away from the blazing ship; a horrified rescue ship saw them right across the bows of the doomed vessel just as two torpedoes came leaping out. The heat must have fired the impulse charges of Quarrie's torpedoes. They seemed to jump out from the M.T.B., flying right over the heads of the Argylls in the assault craft. It was a lucky escape. The Argylls' rate of knots immediately afterwards was incredible to behold.

Then a Messerschmitt came in to strafe the struggling survivors. It missed the Argylls, circled and came back again. 266 picked up half the men, and then another M.T.B., commanded by Harry Wadds, an Australian, came racing over the horizon and picked up the remainder.

Four M.T.B.s were now running together: Smith's, Alec Foster's, and Harry Wadds', with Commander Jermain suddenly joining them. Dive bombers came at them—there was to be little peace for any British ships along the North African coast that day. In their second run, 266 was hit.

A bomb splinter cut an oil line on one of the main engines. The effect was amusing to all except one man. He was a New Zealander, Norman Broad, a weight-lifter with the physique of a gorilla. Norman was aft at the time, directing Oerlikon fire, and he got a shower of fairly hot oil completely over him. He was an astonishing sight, black from head to foot, and more like a gorilla than ever. Only he failed to find it amusing. The broken pipe was somehow repaired, however, and the ships continued at a reduced pace towards Alexandria.

Quite a long while later someone went below and found an Argyll officer lying dead. He was Lieutenant Roddy MacLaren, who had gone below after being hauled out of the water. The exploding bomb had sent a splinter through the hull of the vessel which had killed him instantly. Later they were to find they had over fifty splinter holes in the hull.

There were more air attacks for the little group, but they

kept dodging the falling bombs and hammered back to good
purpose with their own guns, and in time made safety.

Two other M.T.B.s met with tragedy that morning, too.
About 0730 hours, M.T.B. 310 (Lieutenant Stewart Lane,
R.C.N.V.R.) caught up with Roy Yates' boat. Yates was
in trouble, with one engine stopped. 310 stopped a centre
engine and proceeded to accompany the slower craft.

At eight o'clock two Ju 88s attacked them from out of the
sun. They were driven off and no damage was done. For
the next hour and a half they were attacked by pairs of
Ju 88s which came in at about ten-minute intervals, again
without sustaining any damage.

Then 310 saw a single Ju 88 make for Roy Yates' boat
at sea level. They could see intensive firing as the two craft
rushed towards each other; they saw tracer going up to meet
the Ju 88, and realized that it was hitting the plane.

At the last moment the onlookers realized that the plane
wasn't going to pull out of its run. The German must have
been hit. It flew straight into Roy Yates' boat. Instantly
there was an immense explosion as deck petrol, torpedoes
and the Junkers' bombs blew up.

When 310 came in they saw that the wreckage was in
incredibly small pieces, and though they circled for ten
minutes there was no sign of survivors or of bodies.

Eight Stukas came in to attack her. It was a ferocious
battle while it lasted, but somehow 310 came through.
Then two or three groups of Me 109s had a go at the
ducking, dodging little craft, to be followed by half-a-dozen
dive-bombing attacks by Stukas who would not let this one
craft escape them.

About twelve o'clock came the end. It had to come.
The attack was too relentless, too overwhelming. A bomb
landed on the fo'c'sle and blew the deck on to the bridge.
It also blew the bottom out of the ship.

Miraculously, though some were wounded, no one
appeared to have been killed. There were twelve soldiers
aboard, troops attached to the Argylls, and these and the
crew threw a serviceable assault boat into the water. The

ship's own raft was all right, too, and that went in. Water bottles and emergency food kits were brought up on deck. Everything was done at top speed, because the Stukas kept coming back, probably trying to finish off the stationary M.T.B.

Some of the men dived into the water to get clear of the ship. The wounded were placed in the assault craft. A few minutes later the skipper, Stewart Lane, died from his injuries.

All that day they lay on the heaving sea near to where their ship had gone down, men clinging to the raft and boat containing the wounded. No rescue ships appeared. Darkness came. Then they heard an M.T.B. going fairly slowly past them, probably a quarter of a mile away. It was the last boat in from Tobruk, probably Charles Coles', limping along hours after everyone else. The shipwrecked men shouted, but their voices were not heard and the M.T.B. engines gradually died away into the distance.

Then the sea began to get rough. Some of the exhausted men in the water tried to get into the boat, and it overturned and they lost all their food and water.

When dawn came there were only twelve left out of the original total of twenty-one. Tied together, boat and raft drifted towards the coast. Nigel Gray, Stewart Lane's first-lieutenant, was now in charge, whatever that meant under such circumstances. He knew there was a strong tidal set towards the African coast in the evening, and out to sea in the morning. They had a chance of being thrown up on the shore, but that chance had better come quickly, because without food or water they couldn't last long.

Nothing came quickly. Days passed and men grew delirious for want of food and drink. The wounded died and were put overboard. Some went crazy and ended the agony in suicide. Gradually their numbers grew smaller.

On the sixth day only three were left—Nigel Gray, a soldier and a stoker. They were too weak to move.

On the seventh day they saw land. It was a day of blazing sunshine and dead calm, and all the day they drifted with agonizing slowness towards the African coast. If they had had the strength they could have paddled the distance and shortened their agony by hours, but life was almost out of them now.

As hours passed they knew that soon the tide would set out from the coast, and they watched it as if by watching they could hold on to it and prevent themselves from being drifted away from safety—and life—again.

Finally, late in the day, they were washed onto a reef about fifty yards off shore. It took them all their time to fall out over the side of the boat and work their way to the beach, and then they could go no farther. Nigel Gray got twenty yards ahead of his companions and then gave it up. They lay and waited.

Suddenly, on the escarpment they saw a German soldier coming down for a bathe. He was a big fellow, wearing glasses. He saw them and came running down towards them. He simply picked up the wasted figure of the stoker and ran with him. It turned out he was a medical orderly attached to a tented hospital. In a few minutes other figures came running down; enemies who picked them up and tended them gently.

The stoker died. For all of them their agony was ended.

XXIII

ULU was for it and she knew it. She was too near land, and the enemy aircraft would be seeking her out very soon—and would find her.

Commander White crowded on all possible speed, while emergency repairs were instituted. Her W/T sets had been damaged, but were being repaired. One leg of the tripod had been shot away, and the ship holed in the torpedo-men's mess, the wardroom and the chief and petty officers' mess. She was making water in four compartments, but this was easily being kept under control.

In other ways *Zulu* had taken a pounding in the efforts to save her sister ship. There were many dead and a great many wounded. The marines under Major Sankey were working magnificently with the depleted ship's crew, though they too had suffered while under fire.

At 0850 the first of the day-long attacks began. Suddenly a single Ju 88 was spotted. Men ran to action stations, and as the dive-bomber came hurtling in every gun thundered hatred at it. *Zulu* swung hard to port at the last minute, and the bomb missed by eighty yards. The Junkers pulled away, but some thought it had been hit and it seemed to go over the horizon slowly.

But *Zulu* had been found. It wouldn't be long before more bombers sought her out and made more determined efforts to sink her.

At ten o'clock there was a diversion. A surface vessel was sighted to northward. Full of fight, *Zulu* changed course and went straight for the unknown ship, though by now all her semi-armour-piercing ammunition was expended.

When she was five miles away, *Zulu* recognized the vessel as a hospital ship. This was no target for the Navy, and she was left alone. A new course was set, and the battered ship resumed its journey eastward.

Another air-raid warning sounded at 1116 hours. The gunners were waiting for them—seven Ju 88s which came diving at the ship. There was a moment of bedlam, with gunfire mingling with the crescendo of overtaxed aeroplane engines; frantic moments of loading and firing and loading again. The ship seemed to rock over, then steadied. Commander White had taken evasive action. All around *Zulu* great columns of water leapt into the air.

The smoke drifted away. The Junkers were heading homewards again—for more bombs. But *Zulu* had escaped that raid, too. She was back on course again, steaming full out to meet *Coventry*. Once with Force D her worries would be largely over, her captain was thinking.

Not much later Commander White received a signal that was disturbing. *Coventry* had been hit—badly.

At 1234 the hate barrage went up again. They saw six Ju 88s come screaming down at them through the puffs of smoke, saw them rock in the violence of the exploding shells, yet come straight down towards the ship. Then they saw the bombs released. Once more *Zulu* heeled as the helm went hard over, then heeled again as the ship dodged the succession of falling bombs.

And again *Zulu* came through unscathed. Again those bombs only hurt an awful lot of ocean.

Now came a signal from *Dulverton*. It came like a blow to *Zulu*'s captain. *Coventry* had been far worse hit than was first realized. *Zulu* was being ordered to prepare to torpedo the cruiser.

At two-thirty came the biggest, most determined raid yet. Nine aircraft came down upon the speeding ship. Four were Ju 88s; the others Ju 87s.

There was a frantic moment of evasive action, of guns throwing up a murderous screen of bursting shells. Then the bombs were coming down, planes were pulling out over the masthead—the violence of the moment was stunning as the water boiled up all around the ship.

The nearest yet. But the old *Zulu* had out-smarted them once again. She seemed to shake herself free from the welling waters of the nearest near-miss, then go leaping ahead to meet the 'Hunts'.

A quarter of an hour later she sighted *Coventry* on fire. The 'Hunts' were circling her, waiting for *Zulu* with her torpedoes to release them from their thankless vigil.

It was not the best of times for torpedo practice. It meant that *Zulu* had to ease down and swing round to bring her torpedoes to bear upon the fiercely blazing cruiser. And it was at exactly this moment that four Ju 87s and one Ju 88 attacked *Zulu*. *Hursley* and *Croome* were steaming over to give her covering fire. Then out of the clouds dropped more dive-bombers, harrying the supporting 'Hunts' and causing them to look to their own defence.

Yet again superb seamanship and magnificent, intimidating gunnery saved the *Zulu*. The 'Hunts' saw curtains of water shroud her and were certain this time she had been mortally wounded. But again the sleek shape came rising out of the turmoil of a bomb burst ahead of her; she pulled herself out of the troubled waters and appeared to be unhurt.

They saw *Zulu* swing round, reducing speed to twelve knots. They saw her torpedoes leap out and cream across the water and hit the old *Coventry*. There were two explosions and *Coventry* seemed to stagger. She seemed to the seamen watching her like some bemused old creature helpless and harried by those who had been her friends.

At 1505 hours *Coventry*, who had served her country well, flagship of all the destroyer flotillas for twenty years, slid under the waves. Operation Agreement was proving expensive.

There was no time for funeral requiems, however, no moments for epitaphs or even heart-searchings. *Zulu* was being savagely attacked again even before she could turn on course and work up the speed vital if she were to evade the plummeting bombs. Six Ju 87s lashed down at her, wheels seeming like claws trying to grip upon her sleek decks and hold her while she was mangled and torn by their terrible destructive weapons.

Zulu was the target for the enemy aircraft along the African coast that day. *Zulu* had been hurt off Tobruk. They knew it, and they were after her. The order had gone out to the Luftwaffe, 'Get that injured destroyer. *Don't let her get away!*'

But *Zulu*, hit and hurt, was snarling back at her enemies. She was weaving violent patterns in the sea, dodging the falling bombs and stabbing back in fury at the noisy, persisting things that tried to maul her.

The 'Hunts' were closing in, desperately throwing a curtain of fire over the bigger ship. The sky was ugly with little ragged smoke clouds; the day was hideous with noise, and the sound rolled in long echoes over a wide sea that had always seen strife between men upon its surface.

Those watching *Zulu* saw her come riding out of the bomb bursts—safe again. Eastwards flew the frustrated bombers, to load up yet again.

Zulu, the ship that would not be sunk, came tearing along, speed mounting quickly again. When she was travelling at twenty-five knots she held her speed—that was the speed of the 'Hunts', who now closed in to escort her home.

Home. . . . They were moving out of enemy waters now. They were rapidly nearing the area where it would be dangerous for enemy aircraft to venture because it would be within range of our Egyptian-based fighters. Another couples of hours and they could whistle at the enemy.

There were four 'Hunts' left to escort the Tribal destroyer. The other two had gone racing off to Alexandria with the many very seriously injured who needed urgent hospital treatment; their decks were so crowded with survivors from *Coventry* that they could hardly man their guns and were in no condition to defend themselves against further air attacks.

The ships were travelling in line ahead, about a mile and a half apart, *Hursley* as guide to the fleet, *Zulu* tucked in the middle. Time passed; the afternoon was going well.

They were rapidly clearing the enemy coastline. It was almost four o'clock and no enemy was detected on their questing searching radars. It seemed as if the enemy had decided to forget *Zulu* and call it a day.

And then, at four o'clock, came the most savage, most determined attack yet on *Zulu*. It wasn't upon the other ships—they were ignored. *Zulu* was the prize, and this time they were all out to get her. It was as if they had orders: 'You've got to sink her in this attack. It you don't, we won't have another chance. It's now or never!'

It was now.

Eighteen bombers made a concentrated attack upon the destroyer. Six Ju 88s and twelve Ju 87s. They came swarming in from every quarter, giving *Zulu* no chance. They were at her, attacking with a speed that negatived attempts at evasive action. Their bombs were falling so that nowhere was there safety, whichever way she twisted and turned.

Yet even so, only one bomb hit her. Even in such a concentrated fury of attack, *Zulu* came riding through in safety—except for that one bomb.

The bomb hit the ship's side, entered the engine-room and burst. *Zulu* shuddered to the violence of the explosion within her, and then lost speed as her engines stopped, and almost immediately settled two feet in the water. The engine-room, No. 3 boiler-room and gear room were flooded.

Commander White himself went aft and shut off the emergency steam valves to the engine room. When it had cooled somewhat, and the escaping steam had drifted away, he looked into the engine room. It was an appalling sight. Eleven men had died there. The place was a mass of wrecked machinery, but there was no sign of any bodies.

Commander White ordered *Croome* alongside. Including the personnel who had manned the missing motor-boats and dumb lighters, *Zulu* had now lost four officers and thirty-four men, killed or missing while on Operation Agreement. The ship, too, seemed lost.

But her captain was going to try to save her. White

was determined to bring her into Alexandria if at all possible.
He transferred most of his crew and the marines to the
Croome, and then ordered *Hursley* to take the sinking ship
in tow. Commander White stayed with her, keeping with
him two of his ship's officers and nine ratings.

Everyone worked in haste, eyes watching for the next
air raid to develop. But there was a snag to towing, of
course; this was a day when snags just naturally grinned
out at men trying to re-orientate themselves after a series
of events rather too shattering to be immediately assimilated.

Zulu, had lost her wire in trying to tow off the *Sikh,* and
Hursley's wasn't ready. As a compromise, while *Hursley's*
wire was made ready, *Zulu's* large manila rope was passed
and towing began.

Everyone breathed a sigh of relief when the ships began
to move again. There was still a chance of escape, of saving
old *Zulu,* they all felt. They watched the skies, cursing the
enemy who might appear and snatch away their helpless,
sinking ship.

Then the manila parted. *Zulu,* low in the water, was
an awkward old girl to tow. She kept yawing and snatching
at the rope and in time it gave in and broke.

Back came the *Hursley,* the other 'Hunts' circling protectively around, eyes cocked skywards. *Hursley's* wire
was now ready. They got it across; the tow began again.

An air raid developed. Aboard the 'Hunts' they saw
Commander White and his few men and officers run to
the multiple pom-poms and Oerlikons and have a go at
the enemy. Fortunately it was quite a small raid, and the
aircraft shifted away uncomfortably at the barrage that
came up at them.

The tow continued. They were wondering if the last
attackers would summon up a mass attack to finish off the
Zulu and maybe the *Hursley,* almost a stationary target, too,
at the same time. *Zulu* was well down in the water now.
But Commander White obstinately refused to leave his ship
while she floated beneath him.

Time passed. About seven in the evening, after twelve

hours of air attack, a last raid was made upon *Zulu*. Commander White and his men enjoyed themselves with their gunnery. Again it was a small air raid, and again no bombs were dropped. But in the strafing one of Captain White's officers, Lieutenant D. W. Burnley, R.A.N.V.R., was badly hurt in the arm.

Away went the raiders. Night was coming along rapidly now. Not so Alexandria. It was still over a hundred miles away, and the *Zulu* was almost under water.

Commander White reluctantly gave in then. *Zulu* was going under fast. Regretfully he ordered *Hursley* to stop towing. *Zulu* would bury herself without aid from her captain. *Croome* was ordered alongside to take off the men.

The 'Hunts' came almost to a stop as the tow wire was drawn in. They were watching *Zulu*, a gallant ship, about to go under.

It went quicker than anyone, including Dick White, anticipated. Suddenly *Zulu* began to roll over to starboard. They saw the small figures of Commander White and his men being thrown across the deck into the water. Then a white-topped wave rolled over them, hiding them from view as the ship sank under their feet.

Croome, leaping into speed, came swiftly in. They saw heads bobbing in the water. But it took time to get into position to pick them all up. They saw Commander White swimming strongly, another man who had lost his ship that day. Lieutenant Burnley, in spite of his badly damaged arm, was supporting a drowning man. They could see him joking and encouraging him as the life came back into the seaman. Then they were brought aboard.

It was almost dark. The ships began to make for Alexandria. There was nothing now to worry about— nothing. *Zulu*, brave old girl, was gone, and the enemy were satisfied and drinking to their day's successes.

As things had turned out, she had been sunk by the last bomb of the day.

In Alexandria a Wren was greeting a survivor from the

Coventry. She had made up her mind. It was hard lines for the *Coventry* rating, but the boy in the Coding Room had won.

And in Alexandria, too, was an Argyll who was finding no flavour in the half-mug of rum given him on landing at the ambulance-lined jetty.

It was M'Guigan. He was remembering. His money was still hidden away aboard the M.T.B. with the burnt-out decking. The biggest brag he had ever won.

He should have known better than to part with it, with a name like M'Guigan.

In Tobruk Captain Micklethwait was being brought before an Italian naval officer. The Italian looked at the tall, courteously contemptuous British captain and spoke abruptly.

'You were an hour and a half late. Why?'

It was almost the bitterest moment of Micklethwait's life. For the moment gone were thoughts of his losses—his career virtually ended, his ship sunk, and years of imprisonment before him.

A damned Itie was telling him he couldn't bring a destroyer in on time. It was a reflection on his professional capacity, he snapped, and his next two and a half years of imprisonment were to be soured by this bad start.

Big Swinburn was up for questioning, too. This was in another room. The Italians were puzzled, badly puzzled. There was an incredible atmosphere of hysteria about the Italian H.Q. They were quite certain that a big landing operation must be imminent, was bound to follow the night's foray, and they were terrified at the thought.

The thing that kept worrying them, though, was the presence of the trucks.

'How did you get them ashore?' they kept demanding.

So in time Swinburn, a naturally truthful man, told them.

'We swam them in from Malta.'

The New Zealander, Bill MacDonald, saw Swinburn as

he came out from interrogation. He came towards the sergeant-major. The room was full of prisoners, mostly *Sikh* men, but with a number of badly burned and injured marines.

Mac said: 'I thought you were dead, Sergeant-Major.'

Lieutenant Roberts wandered over. An excited sentry shouted, '*Silenzio!*' and hit the big Royal Northumberland Fusilier across the face.

Roberts turned and gave him one punch back. It was a beauty. An interested room saw the sentry fold up. A new sentry was hastily brought in. Mike Roberts, unrepentant, was taken off in chains.

XXIV

EVERYWHERE within the perimeter men were trying to seek a way out. The desert beyond was inhospitable and probably more deadly than the enemy, but no one thought to give himself up—freedom was precious, and while they had strength they would strive to retain it even at risk to their lives.

All day aircraft flew low over the wadis, hour after hour, searching for men curled up in caves and holes, hoping for darkness to enable them to move again.

North of the bay the marines dozed the whole day through, hope growing as hour after hour passed with no sign of the enemy. Long ago the heavy firing east of them had stopped. Lieutenant Harris and all other marines who had landed were already in the bag.

Major Hedley and Captain Powell kept looking westward towards the setting sun beyond the busy road that was the barrier until darkness. Another two hours and they could start, and they were quite sure then they would cheat the enemy.

A shufti kite came up the wadi. It or another had been flying low in and out of the wadi at about five minute intervals all day long. They kept out of sight and ignored it. Major Hedley divided the food and water and organized the men into small escape parties.

While he was doing this he heard a marine say: 'Here they come!'

Hedley joined the marine at the entrance to their cave. Distantly they could see a long line of helmeted men working their way up the wadi. Germans, they realized, heavily armed and far outnumbering the marines. They were searching every hole and dug-out, throwing grenades inside and spraying them with machine-gun fire.

Hedley looked at the sun, but knew the race was lost. There was no point in losing further lives. He walked out into the open with his hands raised. Force A was finished.

Sergeant O'Neill lay up with three men all that day, hungry and thirsty, waiting for nightfall so that they could make a break through the perimeter. The shufti kites were constantly patrolling the area, and at times they saw search parties combing the wadis for them.

When it was dark, they moved. If once they could get beyond the perimeter they had no doubts as to their future. They knew where perfectly good trucks were, with food and water, and they made straight for them.

Suddenly in the darkness there was a sharp challenge. Without thinking Sergeant O'Neill found himself shouting: 'It's all right!' in English—and could have bitten off his tongue immediately afterwards.

Fire opened on them. O'Neill rolled down a slope, losing his companions. He took time off to cut some telephone wires, and then he made his getaway.

But they picked him up at dawn, and the others, too, unarmed, weary, but still game to go on.

That left ten men on the run—ten men who had fought their way cut through the perimeter and were heading for home. Home—Alamein, with three hundred miles of desert and the Axis North African armies in between. There were two parties travelling in roughly the same direction but with no idea of the other's whereabouts.

David Lanark had two men with him: Private Weizmann and a commando, Private Watler. He was making for the rendezvous where either a submarine or an M.T.B. was supposed to come in and pick them up.

Tom Langton had the same idea, too. His party was bigger. It consisted of two other members of the commando —Sergeant Evans and Corporal Steiner—and four men from the R.N.F. They were Corporal Wilson, the Leslie twins and Fusilier MacDonald.

Between the seven members of Langton's party they had a small tin of chocolate, one 2d. bar of chocolate, four biscuits, some crumbs of cheese and less than four pints of water. Lanark had proportionately less for his party.

Ten men, hiding up by day and stumbling over treacherous, rocky terrain by night. Ten starving, thirst-crazed men, roasted by day and almost frozen by night, stumbling doggedly eastward, running into sentries and patrols in the dark and having to fight their way through. Ten men walking through minefields, stumbling into tank traps, and having to crawl naked through the barbed-wire defences.

Ten little nigger boys. . . . A few days later they were nine. Somehow Fusilier MacDonald got lost from Tom Langton's party.

Nine? Eight. . . . Private Watler got lost when David Lanark's party had a brush with some Italians in the dark.

Days went by, then weeks. All the time the two little parties clambered eastwards along the rocky shore line, drinking water from rusting radiators of derelict desert vehicles that made them ill—water from a can in which lay a drowned rat . . . but water. Even sea water.

Once they found a small onion where some Arabs had been encamped, and Tom Langton solemnly divided it and they felt a surge of strength go through them that was incredible and would never be believed by men without their experience.

Occasionally they met Arabs who gave them water and a little food, and even shelter for periods, though they risked their lives to help the worn, starving fugitives.

Seven little nigger boys. . . . For Sergeant Evans succumbed to dysentery and in time grew so bad they knew that only medical attention could save him. He wanted to go on, but they knew it was hopeless, and they had to persuade him to walk to the roadside where enemy vehicles would see him when daylight came. They saw him trudge away into the darkness, his blanket over his shoulder. He was a fine man, the Welsh Guardsman, as grand as any they knew. Depressed, his companions walked on into the desert night.

Seven men who quickly became six. Private Weizmann got shot when he and Lanark tried to break into an Italian camp for food. Lanark helped him when he limped; when the Palestinian grew too weak the Scots Guards officer put his companion on his back and carried him. Weizmann thought him the greatest of officers: always when they came to a minefield David Lanark walked ahead refusing to let the private share the peril. 'It's my job,' he would say. 'I can't allow you to risk your life for me.' Holed up during the long hours of daylight, officer and private ran races with lice taken from clothes found in a wagon, clothes to supplement their own, inadequate for the cold night marches.

Weizmann refused to go on, seventeen days out from Tobruk. Lanark might make it alone, but he never would burdened with the wounded private. Lanark argued, but Weizmann was determined. There was an Arab camp not far back. He would crawl there and seek sanctuary. It was a dangerous thing; Arabs were suspicious of Germans posing as escaping Britishers so as to find Allied sympathizers. Without Lanark, the German-speaking boy might run into trouble.

They divided their food and parted. It was evening, with the last of the light of day on them. They waved to each other while ever they could be seen. It was a wretched, unhappy parting.

And the Arabs thought Weizmann was an *agent provocateur* and handed him to the Italians who gave him to the Gestapo. They tortured him during five days of continuous questioning, beating him into unconsciousness because he would not admit to being a renegade German of the Jewish S.I.G.

They made him dig his grave and once stood him before a firing squad. But always he said no, though he wanted to say yes if only to end the misery of a life too pain-bounded to be worth living. But in time he came before an officer who was not a Nazi. The officer said: 'Do you give me your word that you are a citizen of Palestine?' Weizmann said: 'Yes.' The German officer said: 'I believe you. You will go to the P.O.W. cages and be treated like any other prisoner-of-war.'

Six little nigger boys left. *Suddenly, seven again.* Amazingly Tom Langton stumbled upon Watler living with some Arabs.

One of the Leslie twins succumbed to dysentery. They waited with him to try to get his strength back, but it was no good. Leslie would die without food and medical attention. Once more they had to make a decision. Tom Langton and the others helped the sick man on to the roadside and left him there. Leslie's twin brother stayed with him. Two lonely men were left after a gallant run of over a month.

Five little nigger boys. . . .

Another month of hell and misery. A month that was everlasting and tormenting, during which time they were reduced to skeletons almost. A month no one would ever want to relive whatever the circumstances.

Perhaps there were moments when even they thought of giving in—but not Tom Langton. He was an obstinate man the big Irish Guards officer, a man who would never give in, who would go on long after everyone else had thought they had done enough. Which was why he had won his rowing races—because he didn't know when to stop trying.

Now he kept his three companions moving. He would not allow them to think about surrendering. They had to keep going. They would make the British lines if only they would try long enough, Langton would tell them. His temper was ragged, he was about all in, but he helped, cajoled and bullied his men so that mile followed mile over some of the hardest country on earth—miles that built into hundreds, that must eventually have totalled four hundred and might have been five hundred with their wanderings.

But Langton had grand companions. Tug Wilson, a Manchester grocer who had joined the R.N.F. Steiner

the Austrian, who had renamed himself Kennedy on their
journey because he knew the Nazis had his name from Brückner. And Watler who was uncomplaining, always willing.

They came through. On November 13 they sighted
British troops. They had been two months exactly on their
journey.

On November 18 a British armoured car saw a wasted
skeleton of a man walking out of the desert. He was
bearded, long-haired like a wild man, starving and in rags,
but he seemed quite composed, almost unemotional at
meeting them.

They heard him say: 'I'm Lieutenant David Lanark.'

The last of Haselden's commando had got home. Operation Agreement was finally over.